BAT AND BALL

BAT AND BALL

A New Book of Cricket

EDITED BY
THOMAS MOULT

With Contributions by
NEVILLE CARDUS, D. R. JARDINE, A. P. F. CHAPMAN, P. F. WARNER, JACK HOBBS, R. C. ROBERTSON-GLASGOW, P. G. H. FENDER, HUGH DE SÉLINCOURT, FRANK WOOLLEY, HERBERT SUTCLIFFE, S. J. SOUTHERTON (Editor of "Wisden's" 1933-35), J. A. H. CATTON, E. HENDREN, A. E. R. GILLIGAN, MAURICE TATE, A. P. FREEMAN, WILFRED RHODES, W. E. BOWES, HEDLEY VERITY, H. J. HENLEY, WILLIAM POLLOCK, IVAN SHARPE, FRANK THOROGOOD, H. A. H. CARSON, R. B. ("BEAU") VINCENT, AND A. G. MACDONELL

Illustrations by
TOM WEBSTER, "STRUBE," G. W. BELDAM, "RIP," X. WILLIS, HAROLD GITTINS, etc.

THIS BOOK BELONGS TO
DENNIS O. SMITH
59 GARGRAVE ROAD
SKIPTON
YORKSHIRE BD23 1QA
TEL SKIPTON 795950

FIRST PUBLISHED 1935

COPYRIGHT RESERVED

ISBN 1 85422 700 9

This edition published 1994 by
Magna Books, Magna Road,
Leicester, UK LE18 4ZH
Produced by
The Promotional Reprint Company

Printed in Finland

TO
JACK HOBBS
CHAMPION OF HIS WORLD

FOREWORD

INTO the following pages I have tried to pour something of the true spirit of a game. This spirit has lived and moved on our English cricket-fields for two hundred years, and the pen has done as much as bat and ball to sustain it. Therefore it is fitting that a number of the thirty and more contributors I have assembled, and am proud to assemble, should write as well as play; moreover, they have written with the authority—and, indeed, the sunny freedom—that is in their batting and bowling—and their leadership, for five of the great captains of our time are among them. The only stipulation has been that they helped to make the book one with a difference, and they have, I suggest, responded worthily.

Had *Bat and Ball* not been a book with a difference, there could be little or no reason for its existence. To emphasise that difference I have given importance to certain aspects of cricket and appeared to neglect others. This is more perceptible, perhaps, in the illustrations, from which are excluded some of the subjects with whom the modern cricket-lover has been made so familiar that to include them would be useless repetition. Especially will it be noted that I have preferred the hardly-known portraits of our great cricketers to the well-known. I trust those hero-worshippers who search among them vainly may find ample compensation.

I cannot adequately express my gratitude to all who have had a part in the making of *Bat and Ball*. Their ready help has transformed what might have seemed an arduous task into a joyous adventure, and all that remains to be done by me as I salute them is to hope that the

FOREWORD

joyousness may be shared by those to whom it is offered. In addition to my helpers whose names are on the title-page of this book I thank, for the privileges they have granted and the suggestions they have made, Mr. Edward Chattaway, the Editor of the *Star*, London, who has most generously allowed Mr. Jack Hobbs to contribute, although that newspaper holds the exclusive rights in Mr. Hobbs's work; Mr. W. L. Warden, Mr. A. L. Cranfield, and Mr. J. H. Freeman, of the *Daily Mail*, London, who kindly gave the necessary editorial help following Mr. Tom Webster's characteristic permission to me to make a choice among his hundreds of drawings; The Savage Club, whose menu-card for a Saturday dinner at which the Australian cricketers were guests was drawn by Mr. Sidney Strube—Mr. Strube's gracious response, and that of the Editor of the *Daily Express* must also be remembered as I make this acknowledgment; Mr. W. H. Brookes, who loaned me some valuable photographs (as editor of *Wisden's Cricketers' Almanack*, Mr. Brookes succeeded Mr. S. J. Southerton, (who did not live to see his chapter on University Cricket in print); Mr. J. A. H. Catton, Mr. Hugh de Sélincourt, Mr. P. F. Warner, and Mr. R. C. Robertson-Glasgow, although, being on my title-page, they are thanked already; and Mr. Frank Coles, sports editor of the *Daily Telegraph*, whose co-operation has been uncommonly helpful; Mr. X. Willis; and my day-by-day Press-box colleagues, cricket's laughing philosophers, whose work is insufficiently appreciated for its advance on old standards and maintenance of the ideal once held by Croome, Pardon, Caine, Pullin, Bettesworth, Wilson. . . .

There is also Mr. G. W. Beldam, whose action-photographs have been an *influence* in cricket. Mr. Beldam's life-long love of the game was epitomised in his fine gesture when I asked him to allow me to rifle his famous books, *Great Batsmen, their Methods at a Glance,* and *Great Bowlers,*

FOREWORD

their Methods at a Glance, in which he was associated with Mr. C. B. Fry. Mr. Beldam and his publishers, Messrs. Macmillan and Company, have enhanced the value of my volume enormously.

Finally, I thank my wife, to whom cricket is " a thing of beauty "; my publisher, Mr. Arthur Barker, whose love of the game is half the inspiration of these pages—and thanks also to his partner, Mr. A. L. C. Savory; and Mr. Neville Cardus, my oldest friend in our good world of green fields, summer days, and " jolly companions in white."

T. M.

June 1935.

CONTENTS

	Page
PREFACE	7
PRELUDE TO CRICKET—A POEM	13

Chapter

1. THE STORY OF THE GAME 17
   Thomas Moult
2. BATTING AND BATSMANSHIP . . . 41
   Neville Cardus
3. BOWLING AND THE BOWLER . . . 51
   R. C. Robertson-Glasgow
4. THE ART AND CRAFT OF FIELDING . . 61
   P. G. H. Fender
5. "THE BEST INNINGS I EVER PLAYED" . 71
   Four Great Batsmen
6. "THE BEST BOWLING I HAVE EVER DONE" . 85
   Six Great Bowlers
7. FAMOUS CRICKET GROUNDS . . . 99
   J. A. H. Catton
8. TEST-MATCH CRICKET 113
   Jack Hobbs
9. CRICKET TOURS ABROAD . . . 123
   A. P. F. Chapman
10. CRICKET AT THE UNIVERSITIES . . 135
    S. J. Southerton
11. CLUB AND SCHOOL CRICKET . . . 149
    Hugh de Sélincourt

CONTENTS

Chapter		Page
12.	"THE MOST THRILLING FINISH I HAVE EVER SEEN" *Nine Famous Cricket Writers*	163
13.	SOME PERSONALITIES OF THE GAME *P. F. Warner*	175
14.	CRICKET IN PROSE AND VERSE *Thomas Moult*	187
15.	THE AUSTRALIANS IN ENGLAND: HOW OUR VILLAGE TRIED TO PLAY THEM *Hugh de Sélincourt*	225
16.	A LOVE-MATCH *A. G. Macdonell*	239
17.	FROM THE PAVILION *Thomas Moult*	259
18.	"ANCIENT AND MODERN"	269
	END PIECE: THE NAMES—A POEM	282

LIST OF ILLUSTRATIONS

"Fills our Vision and does not Fade" (*William Gilbert* ["*W. G.*"] *Grace*) . . . . . . *Frontispiece*

                                                  FACING PAGE

The Kitchen at the Bat and Ball Inn, Hambledon . . 12

The Cradle of Cricket 21

A Pioneer of Modern Bowling (*William Lillywhite*) . . 28

The Game Grows Up (Drawing by "Rip!") . . . 35

First of the Modern Giants 46

The Perfect Push-stroke (*W. G. Grace*) . . Between 56–57

The Perfect Off-drive (*W. G. Grace*) . . " 56–57

Jumping Out to Drive (*Victor Trumper*) . . " 64–65

"The Straight Drive completed to Perfection" (*Victor Trumper*) . . . . . . Between 64–65

He Captained "All-England" 71

Beginning the Swing (*Colin Blythe* of Kent) . . . 74

"All the Strength and Pace of which he is Capable" (*F. R. Spofforth*, Australia's Demon Bowler) . . 81

"In his Final Stride" (*S. Haigh* of Yorkshire) . . . 85

A Wonderful Balancing Feat . . . on Toe and Knee in the Slips ("*Long John*" *Tunnicliffe*) 92

Cartoon by Tom Webster (*Daily Mail*) 96

"He Records only the Sunny Hours" (*Frank Woolley* in 1910) 101

"Just Before the Upward Swing Begins" (*Wilfred Rhodes*) 108

"He's a Terror for his Size" (*A. P. Freeman*) . . . 113

LIST OF ILLUSTRATIONS

FACING PAGE

"Ere we Came" (Lord's a Hundred Years Ago) . . 117

The Crabble Ground at Dover (A Drawing by X. Willis, *Kentish Express*) 124

He Scores To-day for his County, Kent (*Alec Hearne Bowling—"Both Feet Brought Together"*) . . 128

At the Beginning of his Gianthood (*John Berry Hobbs*)
           Between 136–37

Champion of his World (*Jack Hobbs, the Great Surrey and England Batsman*) . . . . . Between 136–37

Cricketers' Night (By "Strube," *Daily Express*) . . 145

Preparing for a Drive—"The Movement of the Feet is Interesting" (*Clem Hill*) 149

"Jumping Out and Hitting High" (*J. H. Sinclair, South Africa*) 156

Cartoon by Tom Webster (*Daily Mail*) 160

"With a Bat often as Crooked as Original Sin" (*Charles Macartney*) 165

Cartoon by Tom Webster (*Daily Mail*) 172

The Glance—"Exclusive to 'Ranji'" (*K. S. Ranjitsinhji at Hove*) 177

The Game Began to Grow 192

"Not Merely for Defence" (*C. B. Fry*) 197

"Playing for England" (*Herbert Sutcliffe*). . . . 204

"Father of Maurice Tate" (*F. W. Tate—A Jump before the Last Stride*) 213

"The Modesty of True Greatness" (*Victor Trumper*) . . 220

"A Match of Cricket was Plaid" 225

"This is the Happy Bowler, this is He" (*George Hirst—A Swerver's Grip*) 229

LIST OF ILLUSTRATIONS

	FACING PAGE
" Real Solid Old-fashioned (*Arthur Shrewsbury*)	236
" In Full Swing " (A Drawing by " Rip ! ")	240
A Page of *Wisden's*, 1931	243
Some Old Masters (A Drawing by " Rip ! ")	247
Half-way through the Upswing (*F. S. Jackson*)	250
Cartoon by Harold Gittins (*Evening News*, London)	254
" The Right Arm and Wrist have done the Work " (*R. E. Foster*—Finishing a Hook)	259
" The Croucher " (*G. L. Jessop*)	270
" The Upward Lifting Swing " (*A. C. Maclaren*)	277
The Mote Park, Maidstone (A Drawing by X. Willis, *Kentish Express*)	280

PRELUDE TO CRICKET

BEFORE we came the moon-soaked dews were here,
Washing the feet of thrushes while they sang.
No sun was up when this May morning rang
With the first meadow-music of the year.
Those birds had quired their lovely-throated thanks
To see again the world they knew appear,
The cricket ground, the old elm branching clear,
The daisies on the boundary's unscythed banks,
The green pavilion whose hour draws near,
And (lost ball, six !) the green and brackish mere.

God's praise, Spring sweetness : these, before we came,
Were all : the cool, quiet morning barely stirred.
Now we take on the lease from singing bird,
Assembling here in traffic for a game.
Soon we'll be ready, every man and lad
Tip-toeing, braced how briskly, for the glad
Beginning and the umpire's call of " Play ! "
Busy beneath the hot, slow-circling sun
We'll carry the morning's echo singing on
With its full gracious flavour in every run
Down to the wicket-drawing close of day.
No frowning combat ours, barren of pranks
And genial moves of venture ; lost or won
We'll make it easy, first and last, to find
The clean bright clash of comrades in our match.
All we accomplish, even the bungled catch
Shall challenge joy 'twixt two fresh-flannelled ranks,
Making for summer beauty in the mind
And life's good game when this game's left behind.

PRELUDE TO CRICKET

And as we crowd its setting to the frame
With lightheart laughter and complete content
We'll think, not birds alone had earlier lease
Of these green acres, rich with grass-lawn scent,
And centred in a groundsman's popping-crease.
Even as we pitch our wicket, flickering near
Are shades of men who found this cricket dear
And sealed their happy ventures ere we came.

THOMAS MOULT.

CHAPTER ONE

The Story of the Game

BY THOMAS MOULT

CHAPTER ONE

The Story of the Game

BY THOMAS MOULT

CRICKET is an ancient pastime: it ripened sweetly, it has endured nobly. Ten thousand victories and defeats are chronicled in the game's history, and the smoke of battle never fades from the green field where men and lads have striven with all their skill and strength for the supremacy of bat or ball; but no historian finds himself surveying a more bloodless past than he who writes of cricket. Stern and stirring though it may be in action, so that great crowds of onlookers are often uplifted to a height of wellnigh intolerable excitement (" I have seen men tremble and turn pale at a match," declared the Rev. James Pycroft), the clash is the clean white clash of warriors who can come together and laugh as comrades when all is over, not the frowning combat with a sequel of death and destruction, wrought among enemies. Happy, enviable historian of a world in which rivalry and its attendant envy and jealousy are so fleeting, and everything that is accomplished challenges only joy " 'twixt two fresh-flannelled ranks—making for summer beauty in the mind, and life's good game when this game's left behind " ! Small wonder if those that join in the bloodless conquests of a world whose name is Cricket are inspired with a love and devotion deep enough to astonish the stranger. Long ago the Rev. John Mitford described a visit to Beldham's Cottage, when that veteran of Hambledon and Surrey cricket was in his last years: " In his kitchen, black with age, hangs the trophy of his victories, the delight of his youth, the exercise of his manhood, and the glory of his age—his BAT. Reader, believe me when I tell you, I trembled when I touched it; it seemed an act of profaneness, of violation. I pressed it to my lips, and returned it to its sanctuary." To-day there is many an old cricketer who cherishes the worn-out bat or ball with which he played his part in a famous victory, and he would not be ashamed to show emotion as he handled it; nor, when the cricket lover wanders into some place, like Lord's or Trent Bridge, where the memorials of by-gone days are kept, can he refrain, any more than the immortal Mitford could, from trembling as he touches them. . . .

That such genial labour as falls to the historian of cricket should have been undertaken by many writers during the past hundred years is but natural: and, being a labour of love, it has proved successful often enough for no useful purpose to be served by anything more than a rambling review in this chapter. Time and time again, indeed, have we been told that the origins of the game are lost in rounders, cat and dog, stob-ball, or the stool-ball which Nausicaa and her girls—see Chapman's *Homer*—played in old Greece, playing it, we are informed, " with wrists of ivory," a term which will doubtless be used by some cricket writer when the modern Nausicaas come again into their own. *Again* into their own, I say, because women's cricket was not set on its foundations when their first Test team visited Australia and won a " rubber " for England during the winter of 1934–5. Here is an extract from *The Monthly Magazine or British Register* for October 1811, which shows that however modern the present generation of cricketing girls and women may think themselves, they are merely taking part in a revival:

" A grand cricket match has been played this month between eleven women of Surrey and eleven women of

THE STORY OF THE GAME

Hampshire for 500 guineas. The contest was decided near Ball's Pond, Middlesex. The combatants were dressed in loose trowsers, with short fringed petticoats descending to the knees, and light flannel waistcoats with sashes round the waist. The performers were of all ages and sizes, from fourteen years to upwards of fifty, and were distinguished by coloured ribbons. Royal purple for Hampshire, orange and blue for Surrey. . . .

"The weather being favourable, on the 2d day, much skill was displayed, but the palm was borne off by a Hampshire lass who made 41 before she was thrown out: at the conclusion of the day the first innings for Hampshire was 81, while those of Surrey were only 7. And after two days' further contest it was decided in favour of Hampshire.

"The Surrey side consisted of—Ann Baker (60 years of age, the best runner and bowler of that side), Ann Tayler, Maria Barfatt, Hannah Higgs, Elizabeth Gale, Hannah Collas, Hannah Bartlett, Maria Cooke, Charlotte Cooke, Elizabeth Stock, and Mary Fry.

"The Hampshire side consisted of—Sarah Luff, Charlotte Pulain, Hannah Parker, Elizabeth Smith, Martha Smith, Mary Woodson, Nancy Porter, Ann Poulters, Mary Novell, Mary Hislock, and Mary Jougan."

The records of cricket as a game played by man, woman, or child go back much farther than the year of this clash for cash between the Anns and Hannahs, the Marys, Marthas and Marias, Nancys, Charlottes, and Elizabeths of two counties—how many ladies in twentieth-century cricket bear such homely names? Andrew Lang sarcastically remarked that the enthusiasm of research students had led them to examine the Egyptian monuments and Holy Scriptures, the illuminated books of the Middle Ages, and the terra-cottas and vases of Greece, but " to no practical purpose." It has been claimed that allusions to cricket are to be found in documents of the Plantagenet period, but even if the claim is a true one, it does not matter, because there may be all the difference in the world between an organised pastime and its throw-backs. Adam, no doubt, whiled away some of his golden hours in the Garden of Eden by using a pebble as a ball and smiting it hard with a stick. But that does not make Adam a cricketer.

All we can be sure about is that as an organised pastime cricket belongs to England, the various learned attempts to prove its foreign ownership by a great flourish of such weird appellations as " cricket-a-wicket " (used in Florio's Italian Dictionary) being merely comic. Perhaps it would not be correct to describe as " organised " the particular game complained of by Dr. Johnson in *The Rambler* when he wrote, " Sometimes an unlucky boy will drive his cricket-ball full in my face " (surely the face, not the boy, was unlucky !), or that which was played still earlier at Guildford, Surrey, by John Derrick, gent, who, " aged fifty-nine, one of the Queen's Coroners for the county," testified that " as a scholler in the free school of Guildeford (during the reign of Henry VIII) he and several of his fellowes did run and play there at crickett and other plaies." But the first set of laws ever drawn up for the government of the game, dated 1744, were English enough —and couched in terms pleasant to linger over. (They may be found complete at the end of this book.) " Ye pitching of ye first Wicket is to be determined by ye cast of a piece of Money " : so they begin, and among them we find one ordaining that " when ye Wickets are both pitched and all ye Creases cut, ye Party that wins the toss up may order which Side shall go in first at his option," and another : " If he (ye Bowler) delivers ye Ball with his hinder foot over ye bowling crease, ye Umpire shall call No Ball, though she be struck, or ye Player is bowled out, which he shall do without being asked, and no Person shall have any right to ask him." The foregoing laws have barely changed, and here are others, deliciously phrased: " If ye Wicket is Bowled down, its Out," and (in essence) " Ye Wicket Keepers shall stand at a reasonable distance behind ye Wicket, and shall not move till ye Ball is out of ye Bowlers hand, and shall not by any noise incommode ye Striker, and if his hands knees foot or head be over or before ye Wicket, though ye Ball hit it, it shall not be Out." Umpires were already an institution: " Each Umpire is sole judge of all Nips and Catches, Ins and Outs, good or bad Runs, at his own Wicket, and his determination shall be absolute, and he shall not be changed for another Umpire without ye consent of both Sides."

This epoch-making " constitution " was formulated by the London Club at the Artillery Ground, Finsbury, a place of some distinction in cricket lore, for it was there, in 1743 and 1744, that the earliest matches of which details and scores have been kept were decided. Of course, there are many bare announcements of matches played before that time. In 1700 *The Postboy* advertised one to take place on Clapham Common. And on July 24th, 1705, the following advertisement appeared in *The Postman*:

" This is to give notice that a match of cricket is to be plaid between 11 gentlemen of the west part of the County of Kent, against as many of Chatham for 11 guineas a man at Maulden in Kent on August 7th next."

The same newspaper reported on July 16th, 1720, that: " Last week a match was played in The White Conduit Fields, by Islington, between 11 Londoners on one side and eleven men of Kent on the other side, for 5*s*. a head, at which time being in eager pursuit of the game, the Kentish men having the wickets, two Londoners striving for expedition to gain the ball, met each other with such fierceness, that, hitting their heads together, they both fell backwards without stirring hand or foot, and lay deprived of sense for a considerable time, and 'tis not yet known whether they will recover. The Kentish men were beat."

But such information as that " the Kentish men were beat " or, as in yet another report, " the latter, Dartford, beat the former, the Londoners, very much," is too meagre to be described as detailed, and so is that of the following news paragraph, dated Canterbury, June 3rd, 1727: " We hear from Cranbrook, that a game of cricket was played there on Monday last, by 14 old men of that town, viz.: Richard Shafe 84, Edward Stone 82, John Honey 82, Anthony Comber 79, Simon Dene 78, John Foule 78, John Bus 77, Richard Harris 77, Nathaniel Rone 74, William Cropwell 72, James Bourne 71, Thomas Spice 74. Two old men not coming to time they were obliged to take in Abraham Hitchcock 69 and John Cave 64." Ages and other irrelevances were evidently regarded as of more account than scores, and so it remained until the following summer, when a cricket match was played in the Earl of Leicester's park at Penshurst " between Sir William Gage of Sussex and Edwin Stead, Esq., of Kent, for 50 guineas, 11 a side of each County. The latter played out first, and got 52, and the former wanted 7 to be even with them. It is said this is the third time this summer that the Kent men have been too expert for those of Sussex." To find the actual result still required an elementary calculation, but at this stage the annoyance caused by a news item which reads, curtly: " Wednesday, June 15, 11 Married Men of Greenwich *v.* 11 Bachelors, at Blackheath, for a great sum. Won by the Married," was gradually disappearing. And soon the outcome was being definitely stated:

THE STORY OF THE GAME

"July 11. In the Artillery Ground:

THREE OF KENT	THREE OF ENGLAND
Hodswell	R. Newland
J. Cutbush	Sawyer
V. Romney	John Bryan

Kent won by 2 runs."

Several features of this match (played in 1743) are to be emphasised. The convention of eleven a side was not yet established, but that of omitting a player's initials was already being practised, although its purpose may have been different from that of a later day. Also the match was played before 10,000 spectators.

The earliest encounter in which the scorer's function was regarded as important was played with eleven men on each side, however, and here is a composite report of it, taken from the *London Magazine* and the *London Evening Post* in 1744 (not 1746, as John Nyren stated later):

"Yesterday was played in the Artillery Ground the greatest cricket match ever known, the County of Kent playing against All England, which was won by the former.

"First innings England got 39 and Kent 53. Second innings England got 57 and Kent 44. There were present their Royal Highnesses the Prince of Wales and Duke of Cumberland, the Duke of Richmond, Admiral Vernon, and many other persons of distinction."

The individual scores are printed in John Nyren's *Young Cricketer's Tutor*. The totals given by Nyren do not always tally with those of the newspaper report; and as Nyren has been proved wrong by two years in his date of the match, it is to be presumed that when he copied the scores from the old manuscript lent to him by a certain Mr. Ward, he did not do so accurately. Anyway, here they are, in Nyren's version:

BAT AND BALL

England

	1st Innings			2nd Innings	
	runs			*runs*	
Harris	0	b by	Hadswell.	4 b by	Mills
Dingate	3	b	Ditto	11 b	Hadswell
Newland	0	b	Mills	3 b	Ditto
Cuddy	0	b	Hadswell.	2 b	Danes
Green	0	b	Mills	5 b	Mills
Waymark	7	b	Ditto	9 b	Hadswell
Bryan	12	s	Kips	7 c	Kips
Newland	18		not out	15 c	Ld. J. Sackville
Harris	0	b	Hadswell.	1 b	Hadswell
Smith	0	c	Bartrum.	8 b	Mills
Newland	0	b	Mills	5	not out
Byes	0		Byes	0	
	40			**70**	

Kent

	1st Innings			2nd Innings	
	runs			*runs*	
Lord Sackville	5	c by	Waymark	3 b by	Harris
Long Robin	7	b	Newland	9 b	Newland
Mills	0	b	Harris	6 c	Ditto
Hadswell	0	b	Ditto	5	not out
Cutbush	3	c	Green	7	not out
Bartrum	2	b	Newland	0 b	Newland
Danes	6	b	Ditto	0 c	Smith
Sawyer	0	c	Waymark	5 b	Newland
Kips	12	b	Harris	10 b	Harris
Mills	7		not out	2 b	Newland
Romney	11	b	Harris	8 c	Harris
Byes	0		Byes	3	
	53			**58**	

It was the fascination of this score-sheet that moved the Rev. James Pycroft to exclaim in *The Cricket Field*, his book on the "History and Science of the Game of Cricket," published in 1851, not very long after the disaster at the former Lord's to which he refers:

THE STORY OF THE GAME

"What have become of the old scores and the earliest records? Bentley's Book of Matches gives the principal games from the year 1786; but where are the earlier records of matches made by Dehaney, Paulet, and Sir Horace Mann? All burnt!

"What the destruction of Rome and its records by the Gauls was to Neibuhr—what the fire of London was to the antiquary in his walk from Pudding Lane to Pie Corner, such was the burning of the Pavilion at Lord's, and all the old score-books—it is a mercy that the old painting of the M.C.C. was saved—to the annalist of cricket."

Time has lessened the gravity of that old-time misfortune. Cricket's story since the seventeen-eighties has been one of riches heaped on riches—of personality, achievement, and, slowly grown as the summers pass, tradition. We have all the scores and records we need. We have, moreover, ample evidence of what changes the evolution of the game has involved. We know that the first wicket, comprising two stumps with a bail across them, was pitched somewhere about 1683, as John Nyren recalled long afterwards. Writing in his *Young Cricketer's Tutor*—or, rather, doing what cricketers have often done since, employing another to write it, the "ghost" in his case being Charles Cowden Clarke—Nyren stated that he had been furnished with a small MS., written some years since by an old player, containing "a few hasty recollections and rough hints to players, thrown together without regard to method or order." From these it appeared that "about 150 years since it was the custom, as at present, to pitch the wicket at the same distance apart, namely, 22 yds. That the stumps (only 1 ft. high and 2 ft. wide) were surmounted with a bail."

(In Mr. P. F. Warner's valuable *Book of Cricket*, we are given "an interesting little piece of cricket history" that accounts for these two stumps. " Cricket was originally most popular in the Weald of Sussex and Kent, and there the tree *stumps* were the objective of the man who *bowled* the ball. On the downlands, however, the lack of tree stumps forced the young shepherds to find an alternative. This they found in the *wicket* or gate of the sheep pens, which consisted of two uprights and a detachable crossbar called the *bail*.")

At that period, Nyren continues, another " peculiarity " of the game was in practice. " Between the stumps a hole was cut in the ground large enough to contain the ball and the butt-end of the bat. In running a notch the striker was required to put his bat into this hole, instead of the modern practice of touching over the popping-crease. The wicket-keeper, in putting out the striker when running, was obliged, when the ball was thrown in, to place it in this hole before the adversary could reach it with his bat. Many severe injuries to the hands were the consequence of this regulation : the present mode of touching the popping-crease was, therefore, substituted for it. At the same period the wickets were increased to 22 ins. in height and 6 ins. in breadth, and instead of the old custom of placing the ball in the hole, the wicket-keeper was required to put the wicket down, having the ball in his hand."

Let us use our imaginations a little, and picture the bat used in that game with a hole and notches. It must have been something like a hockey-stick, in order to cope with a ball that required to be bowled along the ground, so that it might challenge the foot-high stumps. When the stumps became " twenty-two inches long, and the bail six inches " as they did in the middle of the eighteenth century " grubs " and " sneaks " were no longer necessary, and the bat would be adapted accordingly, putting on more wood and a greater breadth, eventually arriving at the shape used in our generation. We can imagine also that as the

THE STORY OF THE GAME

bat became less a weapon for swiping and more difficult to beat, the bowler began to use his wits to circumvent it and instead of having to counter the old crude deliveries merely aimed at the wicket the batsmen found himself obliged to cope with flight and length. He met subtlety with subtlety, and thus beauty came into cricket. The Hambledon Club had been formed—about 1750—and as it held a somewhat similar position to that afterwards taken up by the Marylebone Club it is natural that some of its players typified all that was " manly and elegant " in batting and bowling. The game—and the men—began to be glorified, as well as referred to, in verse and prose (previously a poet named James Love had written a well-nigh isolated eulogy), and a later chapter of this volume testifies to the sincerity of those who had a hand in the glorification. The laws of cricket, like its implements, were modified as circumstances required—it was believed until recently that the meeting of a committee of " noblemen and gentlemen of Kent, Hampshire, Surrey, Sussex, Middlesex, and London " at the Star and Garter, in Pall Mall, London, on February 25th, 1774, was the occasion of the first drawing up of a " constitution " ; but it is now perceived to be only one of many meetings at which the original laws have undergone changes.

With the coming of the Hambledon Club and the Hambledon men the tradition that has become cricket's most beautiful and lovable possession began to grow. The old prejudices against the game were forgotten as the fame of Hambledon spread. What those prejudices consisted of we may perceive by turning to an issue of the *Gentleman's Magazine* in 1743, when a writer protests that " the exercise may be strained too far " and that although " cricket is certainly a very good and wholesome exercise, yet it may be abused if either great or little people make it their business." That " great and little " people played together—butchers and baronets—was also a cause of protest. "There is my Lords Sandwich and Halifax—they are statesmen—do you not remember them dirty boys playing at cricket?" So writes one eighteenth-century Etonian to another. . . . Nyren, himself a Hambledon man, must surely have dispelled the last antagonisms when he memorialised the doings on the ancient turf of that Hampshire field. In his pages are the immortal names—immortal because he included them. We read of "Lumpy" Stevens, John Small, Tom Sueter, Noah Mann, George Beldham, "Silver Billy" Beldham, David Harris, and Hogsflesh, and they are more than names.

More than names. Can we not see David Harris "preparing for his run previously to delivering the ball," when his attitude "would have made a beautiful study for the sculptor. Phidias would certainly have taken him for a model"? And in repose also? "He was by trade a potter. . . . His features were not regularly handsome, but a remarkably kind and gentle expression amply compensated the defect of mere linear beauty. The fair qualities of his heart shone through his honest face, and I can call to mind no worthier, or, in the active sense of the word, not a more '*good* man' than David Harris." Then there was "Silver Billy," who "rapidly attained to the extraordinary accomplishment of being the finest player that has appeared within the latitude of more than half a century. There can be no exception against his batting, or the severity of his hitting. He would get in at the balls, and hit them away in a gallant style ; . . . when he cut them at the point of the bat, he was in his glory ; and upon my life, their speed was as the speed of thought. One of the most beautiful sights that can be imagined, and which would have delighted an artist, was to see him make himself up to hit a ball." There was also Noah Mann, who had such agility that when he was seen in the distance coming up to the ground on horseback " one or more of his companions would throw down handkerchiefs, and these he would collect, stooping from his horse while it was going at full speed." Noah " always played without his hat (the sun could not affect *his* complexion) and he took a liking to me as a boy, because I did the same." As for the Hambledon game itself, played week by week at Broadhalfpenny Down, Nyren has paid his tribute in an often-quoted passage, ending : " How strongly are all those scenes, of fifty years bygone, painted in my memory !—and the smell of that ale comes as freshly upon me as the new May flowers."

From Nyren and other early writers we gather much information about the disputes and controversies that have, it seems, always enlivened the game's progress. The introduction of round-arm bowling about 1790, before which date all the bowlers had been underhand, gave rise to an accusation of throwing. " *Protest Against the Modern Innovation of Throwing, Instead of Bowling the Balls* " —such is the heading of one of Nyren's chapters : and, incidentally, a passage in it might usefully be taken to heart by those who put forward their schemes nowadays for reducing a three-days' match to two days. " I am aware," he says, " that the defence which has been urged on behalf of the throwing is that ' it tends to shorten the game ' ; that now a match is commonly decided in one day which heretofore occupied three times the space in its completion. This argument I grant is not an irrational one ; but if the object in countenancing the innovation (and one, be it observed, in direct defiance of a standing law) extend solely to the ' *curtailment* of the game,' why not multiply the difficulties in another direction ? . . . Why not have *four* stumps instead of *three*, and increase the length of the bails from eight inches to *ten* ? "

BAT AND BALL

The " elegant and scientific game of Cricket," prophesied Nyren, " will decline into a mere exhibition of rough, coarse, horse play "—if any except under-arm bowling should be permitted. Nevertheless, round-arm bowling was introduced after much argument about it and about it, and the originators are to be regarded as the parents of modern bowling—John Wildes of Kent, and James Broadbridge and the more famous William Lillywhite, both of Sussex. For a while the authorities banned it, but batting became so invincible that it was revived and became " all the rage," as one historian has it. Higher and higher the arm was raised. . . . Pace developed : Mynn, Marcon, Fellowes, Tarrant, Jackson, Freeman, Hope Grant, Powys, and Robert Long were the names on the tip of the cricket follower's tongue. Then came Willsher ; then Spofforth . . . and lo ! the modern game, cricket as we know it, was in full swing !

Lobs, round-arm, over-arm, slow bowling and fast—each came into use as a result of cause and effect : and so, later on, did leg-theory (or " body-line," or " direct attack," to employ the jargon of the modern period). Nor were leg-guards and batting gloves, forward play and back play, phenomena that, like Topsy in *Uncle Tom's Cabin*, just " growed." They were the batsman's answers when the bowler in his turn got on top. The fortunes of the game swung like a pendulum, in favour of the bat at one time, in favour of the ball the next time. Nothing could stop the movement. " Lord Frederick Beauclerk was bowling to Tom Walker ('a great stick') at Lord's. Every ball he dropped down just before his bat. Off went his lordship's white, broad-brimmed hat, dash upon the ground—his constant action when disappointed—calling him at the same time 'a confounded old beast.' 'I doan't care what ee zays,' said Tom." . . . And King Willow has not cared what any individual may have said. The monarch has been advised, and guided, so to say; but it takes a whole body of individuals to do the advising and guiding; ... with which remark this rambling chronicle arrives at Lord's and the M.C.C.

The influence formerly exercised by the Hambledon Club at Broadhalfpenny Down was transferred to Lord's and the Marylebone Club when, after an existence lasting from 1750 to 1791 or thereabouts, the Hampshire organisation broke up. The M.C.C. became the "Parliament of Cricket," as Andrew Lang calls it, having sprung from the ashes of the White Conduit Club, dissolved in 1787. It was in this year that the first ground of the M.C.C., called "Lord's" after the owner, Thomas Lord, was opened where Dorset Square now stands, and the first match ever played there was between "Middlesex, with two of Berkshire and one of Kent, against Essex, with two given men." The date was May 31st, 1787, and Middlesex won by 93 runs. In 1812 the M.C.C. removed from Dorset Square to North Bank, and, two years later, to the present ground at St. John's Wood, where the first match was M.C.C. *v.* Hertfordshire on June 22nd. Lord was still the owner, and he brought the original turf with him, so that, as Mr. P. F. Warner reminds us, "he who plays at Lord's to-day treads the same turf as the cricketers of one hundred and fifty years ago." Mr. Warner adds: "Since 1814, M.C.C. has grown from a small club to be the most mighty cricket organisation the world has ever known. Its influence is world-wide, it is everywhere acknowledged as the lawgiver and the trustee of the game, and almost yearly it sends teams to every quarter of the globe." Andrew Lang points out in his smiling way that any clubs which please may doubtless arrange among themselves to play *not* according to M.C.C. rules. "But nobody so pleases; and Marylebone legislates practically for countries that were not even known to exist when wickets were pitched at Guildford in the reign of Henry VIII. Marylebone is the *Omphalos*, the Delos of cricket."

The well-known Mr. William Ward, to whom Nyren dedicated his classic volume ("I have not seen much of your playing—certainly not so much as I could have wished") as the most worthy man of the time, bought the lease of Lord's from Thomas Lord in 1825—"at a most exorbitant rate," so that really it ought to have been renamed "Ward's," or "Dark's," for in 1830 Dark bought the remainder of the lease from Lord. During Ward's occupation the pavilion was burned down, involving a wholesale destruction of cricket records, comparable, said Lang, "to the burning of the Alexandrian Library," and moving Pycroft to an even greater extravagance of language in the passage already quoted. A more wholesome disappearance was that of the " men with book and pencil, betting as openly and professionally as in the ring at Epsom," so that " the lovers of Cricket," wrote Pycroft in 1862, " may congratulate themselves that matches at the present day are made at Cricket, as at Chess, rather for the honour of victory than for money." Matches for £500 a side had been common, and suspicion, justified or not, overshadowed the game. " If gentlemen wanted to bet," said Beldham, "just under the pavilion sat men ready, with money down, to give and take the current odds: these were by far the best men to bet with; because, if they lost, it was all in the way of business ; they paid their money and did not grumble. Still, they had all sorts of tricks to make their betting safe." About these " tricks " Mr. Ward said :

" One artifice was to keep a player out of the way by a false report that his wife was dead. Then these men would come down to the Green Man and Still, and drink with us, and always said, that those who backed us, or ' the snobs,' as they called them, sold the matches ; and

THE STORY OF THE GAME

so, sir, as you are going the round beating up the quarters of the old players, you will find some to persuade you this is true. But don't believe it. That any gentleman in my day ever put himself into the power of these blacklegs, by selling matches, I can't credit. Still, one day, I thought I would try how far these tales were true. So, going down into Kent, with ' one of high degree,' he said to me, ' Will, if this match is won, I lose a hundred pounds ! '— ' Well,' said I, ' my Lord, you and I *could* order that.' He smiled, as if nothing were meant, and talked of something else : and, as luck would have it, he and I were in together, and brought up the score between us, though every run seemed to me like ' a guinea out of his Lordship's pocket.' "

The spirit of that shady period was embodied in the Rev. Lord Frederick Beauclerk, who was, we are told, " for well nigh sixty years a familiar figure at Lord's—in his prime he was an accurate slow bowler with pace from the pitch—and his word was law. But, unfortunately, he was as unscrupulous as he was accomplished, and he ' sold ' more than one match. ' My Lord he comes next, and will make you all stare with his little tricks, a long way from fair.' " In this matter of betting on matches the power of the M.C.C. has been as healthy as that of the Football Association so far as soccer on the field is concerned. Cricket in action is as honest to-day as the timber from which its bats are made.

Thus the game grew—and prospered. Old Pycroft actually declares that cricket was generally established as a national game by the end of the eighteenth century, so that its position during the first half of the nineteenth may be readily pictured. The village and the country house, aristocrat and plebeian, alike could boast their proficiency in a game which, crude or elaborate, " was the same in its outline and principal features," declared Nyren, " as the consummate piece of perfection that at this day is the glory of Lord's and the pride of English athletæ."

If a player of a hundred years ago were to return to the cricket field to-day, he would accustom himself without the least difficulty to all its innovations since his time. Before 1883, but not after, each side used to provide its own umpire : that is an example of how slight are the changes. Perhaps the old-timer would stare at our elaborate sight-screens. In the early nineteenth century a sightscreen was often used ; but it was a strip of white canvas stretched on poles five feet high, and this, " while it keeps the stupid spectators from standing in the eye of the ball, provides a white background for each wicket. This is good also in a park, where the deep shade of trees increases the confessed uncertainty of the game. Some such plan is much wanted on all public grounds, where the sixpenny freeholders stand and hug their portly corporations, and, by standing in the line of the wicket, give the ball all the shades of green coat, light waistcoat, and drab smalls."

So with umpires and sightscreens, stumps and bat, already arranged, the scene is set for the appearance of the great players, those whose doings have been properly authenticated. The Hambledon men, the early Lord's men of the type of Osbaldeston and Budd (" who used to go about armed with a three-pound bat, with which he put a ball clean out of the first Lord's "), and those who visited that early Lord's, such as William Lambert, the first to score a double century there—in 1817—must be regarded as forerunners. Alfred Mynn and Fuller Pilch, Nicholas Wanostrocht (" Felix "), William Clarke and John Wisden, Jackson and Alfred Shaw—these were the first of the modern giants.

Mynn was the greatest personality of his era—in more than one sense. He stood over six feet and weighed about eighteen stone : he bowled fast round-arm with an action

THE STORY OF THE GAME

"as smooth as a piston-rod," to quote Mr. H. S. Altham in his *History of Cricket,* and his powerful hitting made him highly popular, so that, as Mr. Warner says, "when not batting or bowling he was generally surrounded by a crowd of admirers, as he walked, bat in hand, round his beloved Kentish grounds in much the same way as I saw Dr. Grace arrive on the Clifton College ground in August 1894. Like Grace, he was a national institution." Born in 1807, in Kent, he played for Kent, and since 1861 "lies asleeping underneath the Kentish grass." Fuller Pilch, who also played for Kent, was one of the masters of batsmanship and is regarded as the first exponent of forward play. "Felix," himself a cricket author, was immortalised in *Tom Brown's Schooldays.* William Clarke captained and managed an All-England Eleven which travelled up and down the country, meeting the counties, but not always beating them. No need to say who John Wisden was! He enjoyed fame as a "very fast and ripping" bowler, but his great achievement was the *Cricketers' Almanack,* which he founded in 1864 and which, since then, has appeared every year.

Jackson, a fast bowler for the county that has given birth to Harold Larwood, was the first cricketer to be noticed in *Punch*. Alfred Shaw, of Notts and Sussex, was not only a slow bowler of deadly accuracy; to him we owe the custom, inaugurated in 1862, of marking the creases with chalk instead of cutting them. Richard Daft and George Parr, whose tree, so called because he made a mighty hit over it, still stands at Trent Bridge, Nottingham . . . William Caffyn and Stephenson, who took the first England team to Australia in 1861—Parr had taken one to America two years earlier . . . grand ghosts, they loom before us—and pass. . . . And then, in 1864, came a cricketer who fills our vision and does not fade—W. G. Grace, for nearly forty years the champion of the world.

BAT AND BALL

The story of cricket since the appearance of Grace is developed in the pages which follow. It only remains to be put on record in this chapter that although the game was played between the counties in the first part of last century there was no serious county cricket before Grace. The inter-county rivalry had previously been a desultory affair, discounted by some of the players being found in the ranks of two or three counties in one season !

The dates of formation of properly organised county clubs are as follow : Northamptonshire 1843 (re-formed 1878), Surrey 1845, Sussex 1857 (although Sussex people may put the year back to 1836), Kent 1859 (re-formed in 1870), Notts 1859, Yorkshire 1861, Warwickshire 1863, Lancashire 1864, Middlesex 1864, Essex 1864 (re-formed in 1876 and 1886), Worcestershire 1865, Derbyshire 1870, Gloucestershire 1871, Leicester 1873, and Somerset 1886. The county championship was instituted in 1873, and this involved the crowding out of the elevens which toured the country under such titles as All England, United All England, and the United South. Of the representative fixtures such as that between North and South, only the Gentlemen *v.* Players match survived for long. It is still in existence. Originally the championship was competed for by eight counties—Gloucestershire, Kent, Lancashire, Middlesex, Nottinghamshire, Surrey, Sussex, and Yorkshire. Derbyshire, Essex, Hampshire, Leicestershire, and Warwickshire were admitted in 1895, Worcestershire four years later, Northamptonshire in 1905, and Glamorgan in 1921.

What has emerged from all the years before cricket reached its full stature ? Grace himself, of course, his black beard, all-dominating presence, and doughty deeds ; the fetish of the " Ashes," symbol of an unending Anglo-Australian struggle, first on English soil, then in Australia, with victory turn by turn ; the increase of professionalism

THE STORY OF THE GAME

as a career ; the decline of the patron and the commercialising of the first-class game ; experimental developments—and failures ; bat and ball in Africa, New Zealand, India, and the Indies ; ever-increasing crowds everywhere : the generations exalting their heroes : Victor Trumper, C. B. Fry, J. T. Tyldesley, Gunn and Shrewsbury, G. L. Jessop, Tom Richardson, Charles Macartney, and Don Bradman ; Jack Hobbs, the master of them all ; and Larwood's bowling, that split the cricket world in twain. . . . The story is a never-ending one—it must be broken off——

And so to the game. . . .

CHAPTER TWO

Batting and Batsmanship

BY NEVILLE CARDUS

CHAPTER TWO

Batting and Batsmanship

BY NEVILLE CARDUS

FOR the purposes of this chapter, batting will mean one thing and batsmanship another. I suggest that the difference between the two words is the difference between utility and art. Cricketers, I know, are certain to prick up their ears at the mention of art (even without a capital A); they will shuffle uncomfortably and say, " Here's the highbrow again—going to mix up cricket with his damned sonatas." Frankly, that is what I propose to do before I reach my two-thousandth word. Deliberately will I " mix up " the delight I have received on the cricket field from great batsmanship, with the delight received in a lifetime from the " highbrow " pleasures called æsthetic. But, I trust, my eye will be kept on the ball, on the technical things that matter.

The crowds that flock to The Oval, Lord's, Old Trafford, Trent Bridge, Leeds, and all the other places, are not as indifferent as some of the lowbrows seem to think to those airs and graces of the game which are useless in the eyes of the scorers and the folk who add up championship percentages. Let us by concrete illustration deal with the æsthetic demands of the man in the shilling seats. We will suppose that Lancashire are playing Yorkshire—at Sheffield, the most vehemently combative part of the country. The position of the game is this: with one wicket to fall, Lancashire need four runs for victory. What a state of things! who would worry about decorative adornments now, in the cockpit of Bramall Lane? We shall see.

BAT AND BALL

Let us suppose, further, that with the agony at its most unbearable, Ernest Tyldesley is defending one wicket and Cecil Parkin the other. My friend Emmott Robinson (would I were with him, wheresome'er he is) prepares to attack Parkin and win the match for his immortal county. He is determined that Ernest Tyldesley shall not get another ball; four to win and only Parkin to " spifflicate." Emmott goads up his shambling energy and lets loose his nastiest ball (" t'inswinger," he calls it). Through the air it curves sinfully and spitefully; it pitches, a perfect length, on Parkin's blind spot. Parkin, quite bereft, performs a reflex action. There is a click and a spasm of apprehension in Parkin's heart. The ball flies off the edge of his bat, an inch past the leg stump, for four. Ernest Tyldesley informs Parkin what has happened and where the ball has gone. The runs go down in the score-books—four runs just the same as if Ernest Tyldesley had got them with a glorious cover drive. The match is over, won and lost. The Lancashire supporters leave the ground jubilant. But before they have reached home they are thinking things over. They are happy that the points were snatched out of the fire for Lancashire. But they say at last, " What a —— stroke ! " And if the Lancashire supporters do not say as much, Emmott Robinson will say it for them. Far more satisfactory had Ernest Tyldesley won the match by a stroke not only worth four, but dignified, masterful, and beautiful.

Cricket, more than any other game, asks for the proud finish of art. The very leisureliness of the game gives scope for individual style. During a long partnership, two batsmen are poised before us for hours; we are soon bored with them if they are merely utilitarians, impersonal compilers of runs. We expect them to perform strokes with a relish and touch of their own. Other games are too dynamic for the cultivation of the style that reveals the man himself. If a footballer keeps the ball to himself for any length of time, in a sudden rush of that vanity which is the beginning of art, the crowd will tell him, with no uncertain accent, to " get rid of it." The cricketer is often doing his job alone in the world—hence the phrase " off his own bat." Here is room for expression, for the personal way of getting a job done ; in other words, here is room for the artist. For my part, I have no use for cricket at those moments when the score-board can tell you of all that is happening on the field. Moreover, no great cricketer has ever lived whose main appeal and fascination did not evade entirely the score-board's powers of observation and assessment. When Woolley is achieving his batsmanship, the score-board is as irrelevant to the genius of Woolley as it would be if it stood at the back of the Albert Hall while Kreisler was playing his violin. No batsman of high class has been content to build an innings much as a bricklayer builds a wall ; he has, consciously or unconsciously, used batsmanship as a means of expressing pride and pleasure in his own notion of how strokes should be executed. And what's bred in the bone comes out in the shortest innings.

From the strictly technical point of view, batsmanship is a matter of footwork. The old shibboleth about the importance of keeping a straight bat has caused much damage to freedom of style. It is good advice for beginners. But few of the noble strokes of cricket can be performed with a straight bat. You cannot cut with a straight bat, or hook or pull or drive to the on. J. T. Tyldesley's bat was often crooked as original sin, so was Macartney's, George Gunn's, Bobby Abel's ; so, to-day, is Bradman's—to name but a few names which will live for ever. The first principle in batsmanship is the position of the feet ; you must be close to the ball, very close, at the decisive second. The second principle (and it is, so to say, a variant of the first) is—use a long-lengthed swing of the bat only to a ball which comes through the air well up to the crease ; for short rising-balls, the short-lengthed, or short-armed, stroke is essential. Here is the whole alphabet, the whole rationale, of batsmanship, as far as it can be reduced to technical formulæ. The rest is personal genius, skill so mastered that it acts instinctively and follows all the impulses of the will and the imagination.

The game will contain all sorts and conditions of people. Stonewallers also serve as they stand and wait for the loose ball. But they must be *vital* stonewallers, stonewallers by the living propulsion of nature. There can be no dull cricket where men are true to themselves. Obstinacy is as exciting, as daring, and infinitely more humorous. Divine laughter comes out of a Lancashire and Yorkshire match whenever a Makepeace gets down on his bat determined not to hit a four before lunch from a Rhodes who is equally determined not to pitch a ball anywhere near the spot where a four can possibly be hit. There is nothing quite so comical as a cussedly obstinate man, excepting two cussedly obstinate men.

I hope my point is gradually emerging : batsmanship is batting plus intense individual absorption in batting. I have no use for the " romantic " school of cricket criticism —that " greeny-yallery " school which gushes ceaselessly about flashing bats. Give me a Collins, entrenched as though behind sandbags, bitter and Spartan, passionately inflicting miseries of frustration on the bowlers and the crowd, as he stonewalls all day for next to no runs, to save Australia from defeat. The virtue of such dourness is not in the draw which is achieved, but in the living humour that comes out of a free unashamed expression of character. Stonewalling is obnoxious only when it is negative ; when it is a sign not of obstinacy, but of the vacant, purposeless routined mind.

BATTING AND BATSMANSHIP

Where there is no vision the game perisheth. Once on a time, at Kennington Oval, England lost five wickets for less than fifty runs on a bowler's pitch. They wanted 263 for victory. Saunders and Trumble were unplayable; they made the ball spin at all manner of vicious angles. They broke the back of the England innings; they annihilated in quick time such great heroes as Maclaren, Palairet, Tyldesley, Hayward, Braund. A Roman innings by F. S. Jackson held the enemy at bay for a while; but it was only a respite. No *science* of batsmanship could withstand the Australian attack on the cruel turf. Spin that behaved so capriciously that even the bowlers could not anticipate its final behaviour—how indeed *could* science deal with it? England were doomed that day so long as the match remained in the world which is governed by the logic of cause and effect. The unplayable ball cannot be countered in the realms of the rational. And so Jessop came forth, chin sticking out; and he took the game out of the stranglehold of cause and effect; he lifted it into the empyrean of melodrama, where the villains are always overthrown. He scored 104 in seventy-five minutes, not by batting but by his faith and his vision. It is beside the point to say that Jessop possessed the technique to knock the attack of Saunders and Trumble off its devastating length, there is no such thing as a technique in the abstract; it is the visible manifestation of the soul of the man who employs it. Jessop's technique that deathless day could not have worked by itself; willpower and imagination drove the machine, lighted the forging fires.

The master of batsmanship speaks with an accent of his own; his strokes ring true. The Hon. C. N. Bruce (now Lord Aberdare) played aristocratic cricket; his cover drives were manifestations of the man's being and of all the fine processes that had gone to the culture of him. The gigantic pull of George Hirst, likewise, told us of the soil and honest homely influences which produced the juiciest of all Yorkshire cricketers. If George Hirst had thrust his front foot elegantly across the wicket, lofty of carriage, and performed Bruce's cover drive, we should have laughed; it would have seemed incongruous —for all the world as though Bruce had spoken to us in terms of " Tha knows " and " Eh, la-ad." Footwork and faith in oneself! Get to the ball, and then deal with it according to your instincts. The trouble with much batting of the present day in county cricket comes from the mechanical standardised formula, the convenient " reach-me-down " and adaptable technique, based on the canny observations of Bloggs of Blankshire, who knows how to stay in four hours on a perfect wicket for 87 not out. Coaching is a curse; no other phrase can express the evil. It is usually negative—" Don't do this; don't do that. Don't try to drive while the ball is new, and when it is old, remember there's a man at long-on. Watch for the wrong 'un; be careful of the right 'un. Don't do this; don't do anything. Stay there!" That is the philosophy of most of the modern instructors of batting: I have heard them.

Who coached Trumper and Tyldesley and George Gunn and Bradman and Jessop and Constantine and McCabe and Hobbs and Ranjitsinhji? They were taught by experience to get close to the ball; their genius achieved the rest. But nothing was done to interfere with the free play of that genius. It was the happy expression of delight in a personal way of doing things. And because delight is infectious, and makes for character, batting was transformed into batsmanship, and cricket became not only a game but a summer pageant, showing the Englishman in all his humours. The noble pavilion at Lord's would never have been built had cricket remained an affair first and last of adding up the runs and distributing the points. And Francis Thompson would certainly never have gone to Lord's and written poetry about cricket.

"You must just put your bat to the ball," said W. G. Grace to a young man who asked him how to play a break-back. The Old Man had no use for theory. He *lived* cricket; he poured his spirit into it, and lo! the game expanded with his spirit. He invented batsmanship, not by abstract argument, but by getting his foot to the ball and taking with it all the heart and gusto and embracing humours that were the man himself. Have I shown yet that there *is* a difference between batting and batsmanship, that the one is a tradesman's affair and the other an affair of the imagination—remembering always the footwork? If there is nothing in this distinction; if it is the mere fancifulness of a writer on cricket, why, then, do the crowds prefer Kippax to Woodfull, or, to take two cricketers who score runs at much the same pace, Philip Mead to Watson, of Lancashire? The one is a character in each of his strokes; the other is an expert in batting. There is an old book called *Great Batsmen, Their Methods at a Glance*, by G. W. Beldam; it contains some of the first action-photographs ever taken, and they remain to this day amongst the best. Look at the portrait of Maclaren making a drive. It is life and energy running beautifully to poise and poetry. It is majestic. Call this batting? No: let us have a more handsome, a more resonant, word. Batsmanship is to batting what poetry is to verse. And I told you, patient reader, that before I came to an end I would get on to sonnets.

CHAPTER THREE

Bowling and the Bowler

BY R. C. ROBERTSON-GLASGOW

CHAPTER THREE

Bowling and the Bowler

BY R. C. ROBERTSON-GLASGOW

IT is my intention in this chapter on bowling to write, so far as I can, a treatise on how cricketers, in the first-class game, *do* bowl, not to enter into a didactic and inevitably stale disquisition on how bowling *should* be done. I think that this method may prove the more valuable, particularly as we live in a cricket age, when the arts of bowlers have been often severely criticised and their very skill sometimes unintelligently belittled and even ridiculed. I mean to write on bowling—for once—almost exclusively from the bowler's point of view.

The bowler has his great moments; a middle stump sent flying with that inimitable and lovely crack of impact; an apparently lost match pulled heroically from the burning; a sticky wicket whereon he turns the artist into mediocrity, the safe plodder into a paralysed novice; but, " for the general award," the bowler is the slave of the game; not often for him the spectators' appreciation, the headlines, the glory of half-inch print; for the most part his life is one of toil taken for granted, of disappointment that, being a bowler, he must subdue, of magnificent muscular effort meagrely—in mere figures—rewarded. If he is a real bowler, he would not have it otherwise. The very nature of his art makes this comparative obscurity a certainty. The vast majority of the crowd cannot see what he is doing or trying to do. The spectators at the side of the ground can appreciate a stump hissing through the air, but not the subtleties of break, of varied flight.

BAT AND BALL

They see a batsman l.b.w., and do not know how or why he was beaten ; a slip catch, and they account it as the batsman's error ; a stumping and the batsman has been too rash ; *always* the batsman ; so *seldom* the bowler !

No need to multiply instances ; just one more will suffice : the bowler sends down a fine break-back ; the batsman lunges forward for a straight drive, and the ball hurtles for four to backward square-leg ; the batsman says, perhaps, " sorry ! " ; the bowler says something else, the wicket-keeper raises his hands in agony, the umpire performs his signal, and 80 per cent. of the crowd cheer—a boundary ; a boundary, not a fine ball.

This, then, is one reason for the slavery of bowling. The crowd cannot see what the bowler is doing. There is another reason, partly consequent upon this. Spectators, in the main, come to see batting, to see their particular idol make a hundred ; attractive batting means gate-money ; money and first-class cricket are becoming increasingly inseparable, and that's that !

There is another, even more important, factor which in these days has made the average county bowler's lot increasingly hard ; that is, the more and more highly developed skill of the batsman, not in making runs, but in preventing his wickets from being hit. This is no place for entering into controversy about the methods of the modern batsman. Too much has already been written about them. But this much is as certain as the progress of the years—his defence of the wickets has increased in sureness and in technique ; the preparation of pitches, purely for the batsman, i.e. for the spectator and the gate-money, has ludicrously outrun proportion and exceeded the original intentions of cricket, the l.b.w. rule is, at present, unfairly in favour of the batsman, with its " benefit of doubt " and its invitation to " covering up " and " pad-play " ; the game is suffering harm from the cheapening of the century and the almost childish attention to records and to averages. When, in a three-day match, the aggregate of runs scored is in the region of a thousand, when an individual fifty becomes of the value of the century to-day, when groundsmen allow nature to have more to do with pitches, and give up much of their marl and their professional pride in perfection, then, perhaps, the bowler will draw level once more with the batsman.

Let us pass now to the methods of modern attack. No one but a man of static obstinacy can fail to see that the whole system of aggression has changed during this generation. The essentials of bowling itself can never change—length, direction, spin ; there have been novelties since the day of W. G. Grace—the introduction of the googly as a foil to the leg-break, the increasing use of swerve ; these are experiments by the bowler, who, being, as we have seen, generally the under-dog, must needs try everything. Being, therefore, experiments, some will become and have become permanencies. The googly will probably remain ; the swerve, as an opening gambit, is at the present moment tending to give way to a reversion to fast bowling. These novelties in individual methods are essentially sane and healthy, though reactionaries may scoff, remembering only the great ones of their own era, forgetting the unnumbered mediocrities. But the greatest change has been, not in such individual methods, but in a whole system of attack which insists chiefly on two things, harmonious variety and its brother—rest with short spells. The tendency in a modern Test team is to include the man who is necessary to the scheme of attack. The great Tom Richardson would bowl away the sunny hours in noble endeavour. It was his greatness to be able to last through a day, and because he *could* last, he was made to do so. Harold Larwood, one of the greatest fast bowlers of all time, is not asked to do this. Concentration and not endurance is the modern system. The bowler is the carefully nursed part of a scheme, not a gallant and heroic slave. From a modern point of view Tom Richardson and his like were " magnificent but not war," the object of a captain to-day being twofold—to keep his bowlers fresh and not to let the batsman conquer any one of them by, as it were, familiarity. There are exceptions to this rule naturally, as when J. C. White bowled for hours on end at Adelaide, and beat Australia, in the 1928-9 tour, almost alone. But the rule remains.

Take, now, two of the most famous attacks of this generation, the Australian team in England in 1921 and the England team in Australia in 1932-3. At the same time we will, for convenience, divide the bowlers into three classes : 1. Shock. 2. Stock. 3. Slow. This division is not perfect, for a slow spin bowler sometimes is used as a stock bowler, and a shock (or fast opening) bowler may sometimes be compelled to exceed his original duties, but, as a whole, bowlers in a Test Match fall into one of these three classes.

Four bowlers should be sufficient in any team ; in the Australian team of 1921 in England the main attack consisted of Gregory, MacDonald, Mailey, and Armstrong. Two fast bowlers, a spinner, and a slow. Gregory and MacDonald provided the Shock, Mailey the Slow, Armstrong the Stock, though at a slower pace than is customary with stock bowling, which is usually provided by a right-hand medium. It is doubtful whether this combination has ever been surpassed for varied excellence. Barnes and Foster in Australia (1911-12) were, in the opinion of many able critics, the greatest openers that the game has yet seen, but those who followed were, though adequate, not of the highest Test class. Gregory and MacDonald were certainly pitted against weaker and more vacillating opponents than is usual, but in their respective styles—

BOWLING AND THE BOWLER

Gregory in the slinging, hurtling, more obviously strenuous fashion, MacDonald with his beauty of rhythm and controlled artistry—they bear comparison with the great fast bowlers of any age. Mailey, to my mind, stands as the cleverest exponent of the leg-break and googly during this generation; his spin was acute enough to beat the bat even on Australian wickets; his flight was subtle and varied, his brain full of device and intent; he never became automatic. Armstrong, as a slow to slow-medium right-hander, was equally persistent, though inclined to be mechanical and unimaginative; he was an obstructionist in the sense that he would fill the leg side with fielders, and bowl to a length on the leg stump.

This was Leg Theory without that personal **danger** which gave rise to the term "body-line." It was not new. W. G. Grace and others had done it with success. With this attack at his disposal, Armstrong was enabled to work out the ideal scheme of bowling, rest and variation; having also two fast bowlers, he was able to "shock" the batsman almost continually. It is worth while to record the kind of attack which he used, and to take, just as a sample, the two hours before lunch on the first day of a match.

(i) Gregory and MacDonald = 40 minutes [12·10].
(ii) MacDonald (10 minutes) / Armstrong (30 minutes) } and Mailey = 40 minutes [12·50].
(iii) Gregory and Mailey = 20 minutes [1·10].
(iv) Gregory and MacDonald = 20 minutes [1·30].

The scheme, though capable of infinite variations, maintained the essentials of (i) short spells for the fast bowlers; (ii) frequent contrast and variety to prevent the "sameness" which makes the batsman's task easier.

The English attack in Australia during Jardine's tour (1932–3) was similar to this Australian attack in so far as the bowling was opened by two fast bowlers, Larwood and Allen. The former went one step farther than either

BAT AND BALL

Gregory or MacDonald. These, following in the footsteps of most great fast bowlers, had from time to time employed the "bumper" or "shock-ball"; it is idle to pretend that this is not part of a fast bowler's technique. To expect a fast bowler to serve up a series of balls on perfect wickets which can be played with a forward stroke or else allowed to pass harmlessly by on the off, is to expect that he should divest himself of the attributes and essence of fast bowling. Larwood, under the guidance of Jardine, introduced that further development in which the batsman, compelled to play the ball, is extremely liable to give a simple catch on the leg side, either close in or to one of the deep fielders standing in the region of square-leg. Obstruction alone, i.e. the removal of offside play, was not new. Danger combined with obstruction was, except in a few isolated instances, a novelty.

That it has been dropped is for the good of the game. Ethically it was the only sane course, but once more it would be well to remember that Larwood was in fact pursuing a policy to which the whole process of modern batting technique had been inevitably driving him; Jardine had realised that Bradman, a consummate master, in alliance with perfect wickets, was as nearly invincible as a human player can be, and Larwood's leg theory was his answer. Ethically it proved to be impossible, but to those who look farther it appears that this quarrel was ultimately and basically the outcome of the increasing disparity between batsman and bowler.

This "invincibility" of the batsman was not, of course, new. C. B. Fry and Ranji in the last years of the nineteenth century and the first years of the twentieth made, at Hove, almost as many runs as they liked on a perfect surface. Consummate ability on a consummate pitch is good for the finances of the game. It results in the crowd-loved scores, the popular hero, and all that. The bowler may break his heart so long as the great batsman breaks the record. A little story connected with these two players is of interest and relevance. A great Yorkshire and England amateur said one day to Ranji, "I could stop you and Fry making these huge scores." "How?" answered Ranji, with a smile. "By packing the leg side and making the faster bowlers aim at the leg stump." Ranji considered for a minute or two, then replied, "Yes, that *would* stop Charles and me to a great extent, but then surely you would never do *that*." And they didn't do it; it was left to a later generation, with the result that has now become famous and has sold thousands of papers and given birth to a flood of books.

So that is the bowler's lot; he has almost everything against him; he goes round the wicket on a wet pitch, bowls off-spinners to a leg-side field, and is criticised and accused of "depriving the game of its beautiful off-side strokes," as if his object was to bowl pleasant half-volleys on the off for the crowd to cheer the ensuing sparkle of brilliance! The game to-day is made for the batsman. The pitch is made for *him*; records are made for *him*; the crowd is for *him* above the bowler and the fielder. But he still bowls, still must speak to his eternally hoping soul—

> Say not the struggle naught availeth,
> The labour and the wounds are vain,
> The enemy faints not, nor faileth,
> And as things have been, they remain.

And *will* remain, too, until a more enlightened legislature choose to give concrete effect to what all real cricketers in their hearts know, to restore the balance between him and the batsman, to give back to the game that which it once possessed on the downs of Hambledon when money and cricket were still far apart.

* * * * *

BAT AND BALL

Soon after this chapter was written, M.C.C. made two moves of high importance. First, they ruled that any method of bowling which, in the umpire's opinion, constitutes " a direct attack on the batsman standing clear of his wicket " is unfair. Secondly, they decided to experiment with a new l.b.w. rule, the effect of which was to cause the batsman to be out if he stop with his legs or body, *when they are on the line between wicket and wicket*, a ball that pitches outside the off stump and would have hit the stumps.

As to the first move, in the matter of Fast Leg Theory, so much has been written and said—far too much—that I would only add here that the sooner ill-tempered, vicious, and merely " commercial " bowling ceases, the better for the game. Every cricketer knows such bowling when he sees it ; would that all others knew it for what it is, a blot on the game !

As to the experimental l.b.w. rule, it was worth trying, but I much doubt if it will stay. I think that umpires have not found it difficult to administer, but it has led already to such queer results that cricketers will almost unanimously wish to discard it.

To return to our original theme, the over-perfection of modern pitches. That is the chief root of modern evils in cricket. Return to pitches on which an average score of 250 would be made, and we would never need either Fast Leg Theory or a change in the l.b.w. rule.

But crowds (and newspapers) love centuries and record totals ; crowds mean money, and without money County Cricket cannot exist. It is the old, old struggle between Mammon and Art.

CHAPTER FOUR

The Art and Craft of Fielding

BY P. G. H. FENDER

CHAPTER FOUR

The Art and Craft of Fielding

BY P. G. H. FENDER

WHILE it must be conceded that, most of the time, fielding is the least spectacular part of cricket, it is, in the opinion of many who play the game, the most important of the three categories into which the practice of the game is divided. Batting may provide the thrills, and claim the eye to the greatest extent, but an accident may at any time happen to a batsman. That is to say, he may, right at the start, or at any moment after the start of his innings, run into the unplayable ball, or one of the other unforeseen and unavoidable happenings, which puts an end, summarily, to his life at the crease, or he may make a mistake.

Bowling is, normally, less spectacular from the onlookers' point of view, if only because those on the ring-side can see so little of what the bowler is really doing, unless he is hitting the stumps or causing the batsman to mis-hit the ball. Fielding, on the other hand, is more nearly understandable to any one, or all, of the spectators all the time, and it is a well-worn and very true phrase, that good fielding can make bad bowling into moderate bowling, and moderate bowling into good bowling, and good bowling into superlative bowling.

Of the three great departments of the game, there is one thing which can be said without any fear of contradiction, and that is that in fielding alone, of the three, proficiency can be achieved by anyone.

Any player, who is keen enough, can learn to be a good

field, even if he cannot achieve genius; it only needs a willing heart in the face of hard work, and a moderate intelligence, to enable a player to be a good, sound, and reliable field, though perhaps a little more may be needed to earn a reputation as a really great fielder.

Fielding itself is of course divided into three main categories—catching, throwing, and ground fielding—and though the first can be practised and, in every individual case, improved, it is certainly the one in which the matter of genius may enter more than either of the others. Throwing can be practised, and, with a competent coach, there are few who cannot become proficient, if not very good throwers. Ground fielding, or perhaps some may call it stopping, can certainly be learnt by practice, and with the aid of a few hints as to the natural antics of the ball in certain circumstances and the best way to use the hands, a very high degree of proficiency should accompany courage.

Naturally, experience is a big factor in any of the branches of fielding, for only of experience can anticipation be born, and, once the player is past a certain stage of proficiency in his efforts to learn the rudiments of fielding, intelligent anticipation is probably the chief difference between the good, sound, hard-working fielder and the genius.

Of course, in writing of cricketers and fielding, I am presupposing the possession, by those who read me, of the rudimentary necessities in a cricketer before he makes any attempt to start to play the game.

By that I mean that I take it that the reader for whom I write is possessed of a sound body, of reasonable physique, and an eye of reasonable speed and clarity. A cricketer, to become at all proficient, must be possessed of these advantages; all the others he can learn or achieve, in a greater or less degree, by practice.

THE ART AND CRAFT OF FIELDING

Now, to take the three departments of fielding one by one, let us start with throwing. I am well aware that there are players who, whatever their other abilities may be, are constitutionally unable to throw well. There are such, and incidentally, I, myself, am one of them, but they are few and far between, and even I might have been a good thrower had I given a certain amount of time to throwing in my early days as a youngster in the game. The fact that I did not do so was due partly to my having, almost since the start of my cricket life, fielded in the slips, and consequently overlooked, in the early days, the necessity for equipping myself for throwing. One has only to give a moment's thought to baseball to realise how proficient at throwing almost anyone can become by dint of assiduous practice. One seldom, if ever, sees a cricketer standing out in the field with a companion practising throwing, and doing it by easy stages. That is to say, throwing a ball comfortably and quietly, backwards and forwards with his companion, over a short distance to start with, and gradually, as proficiency increases, lengthening the distance of the throw.

You see that being done for half an hour at a time before a baseball match, by the players who are going to play in the match and their reserve players. One can do a tremendous lot to improve one's throwing by such methods, both from the point of view of exercising the particular muscles required for throwing, and for accuracy and speed.

Those who know Jack Hobbs well on the field will remember that he used to take every possible opportunity of throwing the ball hard and straight at either Strudwick or Brooks at the fall of a wicket, or even on the occasions when the last ball of the over was played to his hands at cover. Practically any player can become a good thrower if he starts early enough in his cricket life, and practises often and hard enough all through.

BAT AND BALL

The next important part of fielding is, of course, the ground fielding, or stopping. The things necessary to success in this department naturally vary with the different positions in the field occupied by the individual. Fielding in the slips is, in my opinion, something apart from fielding in any other position, so I will leave that for a few words later, in its special category. Broadly, the matter of ground fielding in other positions requires, in the fielder, a sound judgment of speed and sometimes of the flight of the ball, a good stout heart, and an ability to concentrate his mind on the ball as it comes towards him. In certain positions he has to learn the peculiarities which are linked with particular bowlers, for, especially at third man, the ball will retain, as it comes towards the fielder, some of the spin imparted to it either by the bowler, or by the batsman in the course of making the stroke. In the main, a fielder at third man for a right-hand batsman will always find that a ball coming to him along the ground, or in short sharp bounces, will tend to curl, to a greater or less degree, to his, the fielder's, left. The ball seldom takes a bias to the right, so that a fielder in this position would usually meet the ball, as it approaches him, a little on the left of the apparent line of flight.

In this manner he is ready for any sudden curl to that side which, if it occurs when he is unprepared, may make him mis-field the ball, and will certainly, if he does not miss it, cause him to pick it up with his left hand, and, unless he is a left-handed thrower, lose time in his return to the crease. At cover, the curl, if any, will also usually be towards the left, though there are times when, if the batsman, in making his stroke, " stuns " the ball, it will take a very odd jump to the right. Experience alone will enable the fielder to anticipate such things. At mid-off or mid-on, the work is more or less straightforward, and the qualities required of the fielder are little more than a good

THE ART AND CRAFT OF FIELDING

heart, no flinching, and an ability to keep his eye on the ball. Fielding in the country, whether on the straight drive, on the deep-leg boundary, or at deep extra cover, is quite a different matter to occupying any other of the positions in the field. Whether the ball is coming along the ground or in the air to him, the player in these positions must have something which is not usually demanded of those in any of the other positions. He must cultivate the ability, when the ball is coming, to exclude from his mind, and from his senses, all other things than the ball itself, and the ball alone. It does not happen so often in the minor grades of cricket as it does the higher you progress up the scale in the game, but in almost every case it happens to a greater or less degree that the fielder in the country risks being interfered with, in his work, by the presence of, or shouts from, spectators.

Such things can be very disturbing to the fielder, but, if he wishes to play big cricket, he certainly must cultivate the ability to ignore and completely exclude such outside influences. Naturally, the fielder in the country must be a good runner, a safe catch (and that can come from assiduous practice), and a good thrower ; and he must also, if it is possible, cultivate a certain sense which will enable him to know, without looking, the end to which he can most advantageously return the ball when he has fielded it. This sense can be gathered by permitting in his subconscious mind, as the ball is coming towards him, or he is running after it, a species of judgment of where the batsmen will be, in running between the wickets, at any given moment, always bearing in mind anything he may have seen, before concentrating on the ball, of a late start by one or the other batsman.

Fielding near the wicket, that is to say, in the slips, at short-leg, or near behind the wicket on the leg side, is something for which some are born, and others are not.

BAT AND BALL

Anyone can learn to field well in all the deep positions or in front of the wicket, though naturally some are better than others, but all are not able to field in the close positions. In such places success is very largely a matter of instinct. One can help any such instinct by watching the bowler and then the stroke which the batsman is making, as well as keeping an eye on the ball as the bowler delivers it, and experience also plays a big part, but everything in such positions is so much a matter of a snap chance, with little or no time to think consciously, or to appreciate the facts which one's eye has seen, that the instinct is either there or not there, and that can very soon be decided upon by the individual or his companions. No one can say till well afterwards how a sharp chance in the slips or at short-leg was taken.

The fielder himself will have a very hazy idea of the course of events at the actual moment, though, after it is all over, and the catch or stop has actually been made or missed, he will almost certainly receive in his brain an accurate impression of what happened. That is a matter of the muscles having acted without there being time for a conscious impression to have been received in the mirror of the brain, and therefore fielding in such positions will be largely a matter of instinct, coupled with experience.

I have often been asked whether I watch the ball from the bowler's hand or from the bat when I am fielding, and I think that one can quite definitely suggest that there are great advantages in watching the ball from the moment when it leaves the bowler's hand, in every position where it is possible to do so without altering the position of one's head.

Naturally, the eyes take time to focus the ball again if one moves one's head while the ball is in flight, and therefore it is of the greatest possible advantage to move one's head as little as possible when concentrated on the ball.

THE ART AND CRAFT OF FIELDING

That accounts for the fact that a catch in the country is missed more often when the fielder is running than when he is able to stand and steady himself before the arrival of the ball. On this basis I would therefore suggest that at silly-point or short-leg, in front of the wicket, and such positions, the ball must be watched off the bat, but in all others where it is possible, it should be watched from the bowler's hand.

There are, of course, a great many other things about fielding upon which, in the space at my disposal, I am unable to touch, but I hope that I have made it clear that all players of the game can become good fielders, even if not great ones, by means of a little concentrated effort. None need write themselves off as impossible, for a little application can always make them presentable.

I hope that some of the things I have written may have provided for others one or two different angles from which to view the most important department of the game.

CHAPTER FIVE

"*The Best Innings I ever Played*"

BY FOUR GREAT BATSMEN

1. ... AND MY BIGGEST DISAPPOINTMENT
    BY FRANK WOOLLEY

2. ON A STICKY WICKET AT MELBOURNE
    BY HERBERT SUTCLIFFE

3. TEN RUNS IN HALF AN HOUR ...
    BY E. ("PATSY") HENDREN

4. "A HUNDRED ON SUCH A WICKET WOULD BE WONDERFUL ..."
    BY D. R. JARDINE

CHAPTER FIVE

" *The Best Innings I ever Played* "

BY FOUR GREAT BATSMEN

. . . AND MY BIGGEST DISAPPOINTMENT

BY FRANK WOOLLEY

IN the second Test Match of 1921, at Lord's, I made 95 and 93 in my two innings for England against Australia.

I shall always regard these as my best achievement. I never batted so strongly, I never cut so hard or hit to square leg for such lightning boundaries. And yet I came to the wicket when England were facing heavy odds, especially in the second knock. We had been beaten by ten wickets at Nottingham, and already the Australians looked like sweeping everything before them in the Tests.

Not only had they the three deadliest bowlers of the day —Gregory and Macdonald, than whom I have never encountered a better pair, Macdonald being the best fast bowler I have played against and a yard faster than anyone else ; and Mailey, with his googlies and leg-breaks. But I do not remember a fielding side of their standard. Charles Macartney, for example, was at deep-third man, and Pellew, the long-leg, covered the ground so swiftly that I was not surprised to learn he had done a hundred yards in even time.

I think I must have worked harder for my runs in those two innings than I have ever done. I felt wonderfully fit, and even able, given proper support, to have turned the scale of England's fortune. But I had the great disappointment of just missing my hundred in each innings—by 5 runs in the first and by 7 in the second!

On the opening morning I went in first wicket down, when England were 20 for the loss of D. J. Knight. Soon the score was 25 for three, with Dipper and Hendren out as well. Only that big-hearted fighter, "Johnny" Douglas, stayed in with me, and we lost nine wickets for a paltry 170. Eight batsmen had made 38 between them!

Jack Durston joined me as last man in. Of course, I tried to keep the bowling. Four times I hit Mailey hard, but we did not go for the singles. To his fifth delivery—a rank long-hop—I walked down the pitch and tried to drive through the covers. I missed the ball completely and was stumped.

In the second innings England, 155 behind, did rather better. Dipper and Lionel—now Lord—Tennyson got runs, and again I came within sight of my century. But I was out to another of Arthur Mailey's bad balls—caught by Hendry, rolling over and over. That was on the Monday. I can only think of one occasion in all my career that caused me such disappointment—and that was on the Saturday!

ON A STICKY WICKET AT MELBOURNE

BY HERBERT SUTCLIFFE

Not by any means the best judge of his own performances is the player himself, and many people will have decided that in the Oval Test of 1926, between England and Australia, I had my best innings. But I look back with more satisfaction to the third Test Match at Melbourne during the 1928–9 tour than I do to any other innings I have played.

"THE BEST INNINGS I EVER PLAYED"

The game resolved itself into one of those grim, fluctuating struggles so familiar in Australian cricket. It lasted for a week, and was full of thrilling moments. Batting first, Australia scored 397, to which England replied with 417. Hammond was our top scorer: he made exactly 200. The second Australian knock resulted in a score of 351, and England were left with 332 to get for victory.

On the sixth night Dame Fortune played us a vile trick in the shape of a terrific thunderstorm, which sent our hopes to zero. For our arrival at the ground brought the swift realisation that our task was indeed a super-task. Many Australian experts, including Noble, Armstrong, Mailey, and Macartney, were of the opinion that England would do well to score 80! And indeed, the wicket on which we had to bat is reputed to be the worst type of sticky wicket in the world.

Jack Hobbs and I discussed the possibilities as we walked out to open the innings, and we both agreed that it would be a magnificent day's work if our side could make more than 80. However, the unexpected happened, and after Hobbs had been missed in the slips off one of the first few balls, we gradually settled down to one of the most intense and amazing fights of my career.

In some miraculous manner we managed to pass the hundred for the first wicket. After Jack left—with a score of 49—Douglas Jardine filled the breach as only a cricketer of his skill and great fighting temperament could. Even after Hobbs had gone the wicket remained bad, and Jardine's 33 was worth at least 120.

Eventually we began to see success in front of us, and in the end we won by three wickets—a most unexpected victory after the storm had reduced us to despair.

[EDITOR'S NOTE.—Sutcliffe made 135. He had batted nearly six and a half hours and was fourth out, when England needed only 14 to win.]

BAT AND BALL

TEN RUNS IN HALF AN HOUR

BY "PATSY" HENDREN

Time dims the memory. Hence I do not go very far back for an innings which, considering all the circumstances, I consider certainly the most trying, even if the word "best" cannot rightly be applied to it. It only lasted, really, for half an hour on the second day of the Test Match played at Nottingham in the summer of 1934.

Consider the circumstances. When the season started, I had not the faintest idea that I should again be called upon to play for England. In due course, however, I was selected, at the age of forty-five. Australia batted for most of the first two days, putting up a total of 374. I was Number Six on the batting list, so that when the clock had already turned towards six and we were only one wicket down, I felt justified in starting to change into my "civilian" attire. But then came a disastrous twenty minutes for England, and I was going out to bat as the clock struck six. Four England men were out for 114, and there was still half an hour to go before closing time.

The Australians had never expected to be in such a good position; Grimmett and O'Reilly were bowling like demons; the fielders were clustering round the wicket. Never in my career have I spent such a complete half-hour on the rack. If only the Nawab of Pataudi and I could stay there till stump-drawing, England had a chance.

We managed to do so, as it happened, the huge crowd watching in a painful silence every ball sent down. How I had the pluck to sweep Grimmett round to leg for two fours I don't know even now! I only scored 2 more runs—10 altogether—in that half-hour, while the Nawab's contribution was 3. But we were still together—to start again on Monday morning. Need I add that the waiting through the week-end for Monday was almost as bad as

"THE BEST INNINGS I EVER PLAYED"

that tense last half-hour on Saturday? As my old friend Clarrie Grimmett truly said: "Pat, you're too old for that sort of ordeal."

"A HUNDRED ON SUCH A WICKET WOULD BE WONDERFUL. . . ."

BY D. R. JARDINE

I

To say that it is a matter of considerable difficulty to select the best innings one has ever played should not be misunderstood by a charitable reader. It does not imply that the field of choice is distressingly large, as would be the case if the question was one of choosing the *worst* innings one has ever played! Rather the difficulty lies in holding the scales evenly between the quality of the opposition encountered on different occasions, and the easiness, or the reverse, of the conditions under which any particular innings was played.

This, one may as well confess, is wellnigh impossible. I am tempted to digress to the extent of saying that those who imagine that the worst innings imaginable terminates abruptly with the first ball the batsman receives are in many cases very wide of the mark. Common honesty and clear thinking alike must compel us to admit that there must be a line drawn, clearly distinguishing the occasions upon which the bowler gets the batsman out, and the times when the batsman gets himself out. To throw one's wicket away needlessly, and to the detriment of one's side, must be an essential element in the worst innings any of us have ever played.

As a solution to the difficulty of making the choice, I would suggest that if an innings in some degree satisfies on three main points, it is likely to be our best. Firstly,

BAT AND BALL

then, if it was played at a time when a good deal depended upon it, it will satisfy us as individuals. Secondly, if played under conditions favourable to the bowlers, it will satisfy us as batsmen. Thirdly, if the course pursued was dictated by the needs and interests of the side, it will appeal to us as cricketers.

The setting and the conditions together furnish more than half the interest such as it may be : while frankly the doings of two other batsmen supply nearly all the remaining interest, together with a proportionate share of any kudos there may be.

II

The scene, dramatically enough, is laid in Melbourne during the M.C.C. tour of 1928–9. It is the third Test Match of the series of five, and England has already won the two previous matches.

Three hundred runs is a formidable score to face in the fourth innings of any match, but the 320-odd runs which England needed did not seem at all an impossible task. Had not Hammond made 450 runs in his last two innings against Australia ?

All this, however, without reckoning on the weather playing any scurvy tricks. During the night a third of an inch of rain fell. Various grounds under such conditions have sinister reputations, differing only in degree. None, by common consent, so ominously sinister as Melbourne. Under similar conditions Rhodes, I think, took fifteen wickets in a Test Match, and capped this by bowling all Victoria out for 12 runs. On the latter occasion one batsman, who ultimately made three-quarters of his side's total, was dropped off a " sitter " before he had scored !

Even such as myself, who had never seen an Australian sticky wicket, knew that it was " a hundred to a hay seed "

"THE BEST INNINGS I EVER PLAYED"

that the rain had spelt good-bye to any hopes we might have cherished of winning the rubber straight of the reel. A deal of the pleasures of retrospect are bound up with a realisation of how different realities prove from anticipations. Glorious mornings breed confidence and hope in the batsman's heart, best illustrated by two of A. A. Milne's delightful characters at breakfast on a fine summer's morning if my recollection serves.

" 'By Hobbs, I shall make a century to-day!'

" 'You will make exactly seventeen' (this from Myra).

" 'It sounds a lot,' said Archie."

On the dull morning of which I write, it would have been a bold batsman who fancied his chances of making seventeen.

III

We found when we arrived at the ground that it was quite unfit for play. But shortly before lunch and after the captains had disagreed, the umpires decided in favour of Ryder. Australia had still two wickets in hand, but in spite of the ball being like a piece of wet soap, these wickets only added about 4 runs. The batsmen rightly refrained from patting down the chunks raised by each ball which pitched on the wicket. England were left with ten minutes' batting before lunch. Some idea of how wet it was may be gathered from the groundsman's explanation of why he did not give the wicket the full time of rolling prescribed. When asked next morning, he said that the roller was beginning to lift bits off the top of the wicket. Hobbs and Sutcliffe made one run in the trying ten minutes before lunch, without being separated.

Lunch was scarcely a cheerful meal for the English team, faced with the prospect of playing the part of ninepins, and being rapidly skittled. On the way I met Mr. Hugh Trumble, one of the greatest, as well as the most charming, of a different generation of Australian cricketers. As secretary of the Melbourne Cricket Club (familiar initials M.C.C.) Mr. Trumble was popularly supposed to know each blade of grass on the ground by name and number. He was good enough to begin by sympathising with our side's bad luck—with which I naturally agreed, but added words to the effect that it wasn't all over yet by any manner of means. Hope dies hard, but Mr. Trumble did his best to shatter any remnants, by countering with : " Maybe not, but it will all be over by teatime."

He was quite serious, and in fairness be it said, that in his prime he himself would have been quite capable of bowling all England out between lunch and tea. He speculated further that we should make between 50 and 70 runs—a total of 100, he said, on such a wicket would be a wonderful batting feat, little short of a miracle.

Further proof of the general view, if any was needed, was furnished by a member of the Australian eleven. I had not had an earlier opportunity of congratulating him on his innings the day before. He vouchsafed the information that all Australian wickets under the circumstances would be sheer glue-pots, but that the Melbourne wicket stood out in a class by itself. " She's a fair snifter ! " he added. Very soon after the interval, the ball began to play a series of alarming tricks.

The ground, which before lunch had boasted a bare two or three thousand spectators, was rapidly filled up by the influx of at least twenty thousand. Said an Australian, talking to Mr. Fender, who was out there as a special correspondent : " You didn't know we had fox hunting in Australia, did you ? " Mr. Fender was justifiably puzzled and said, " No. Why ? " For answer, his friend pointed at the crowds surging in, with the words, " Look at them hurrying up to be in at the death ! "

IV

A word about the differences between sticky wickets in England and Australia. The ball in England under such conditions turns, and does so quickly enough in all conscience, but there is a certain uniformity both in respect to the pace and the height at which it does so. In Australia it is " quite otherwise." In the course of a single over it would not be unusual for one ball to shoot, two to turn like greased lightning, and three to lift shoulder high. The batsman, in Australia, labours under one further disadvantage in that the bowler's footholes allow of a fast bowler bowling, where in similar circumstances in England he would slip and fall.

The best-length ball any bowler, be he fast, medium, or slow, can bowl on these wickets is probably a ball just short of a half-volley—the wicket will do the rest.

Momentarily we in the dressing-room were expecting a wicket to fall. Number Four on our batting order expressed surprise that I was not padded up—a queer thought considering the four names which preceded mine in the list. I felt that it would be bad for " moral " if Number Five padded up. In most respects Australian grounds are superior to English, but the dressing-room accommodation is atrocious—the mere players presumably being of even less account than is the case in England, compared to the authorities who control the game. From our dressing-room only three people could sit and watch the play.

Hobbs and Sutcliffe, as was inevitable, were making heavy weather of it—and yet if one lapse be excepted, they seemed to command the situation in some degree three-quarters of the time. This is not to say that runs were easy to get, or indeed were got at any pace. Nor does it imply that the batsmen were not beaten and hit frequently by the ball. They were, in fact, hit from the neck downwards, but these were pre-leg-theory days! though Blackie's field at one time boasted only three men on the off-side—one of whom was quite wasted. The one exception was when Hobbs early on was dropped by Hendry at slip. An expensive blunder.

v

Any spectator who was fortunate enough to see the same batsmen bluff Collins and Richardson at The Oval in 1926 would have revelled and marvelled at a precisely similar repetition of the feat in Melbourne, if Ryder and Blackie be substituted for the former names.

The batsmen took a chance on anything short, and a series of powerful hooks forced an array of square-legs to such a respectful distance, that they could not snap up the quick close chance which lifts off the bat from a fast-rising good-length ball. Yet all this would have gone for nothing if only the off stump instead of the leg stump had been attacked—this whether the bowler on such a wicket bowled over or round the wicket with his off-breaks. At The Oval Hobbs eased his task, while minimising the dangers from the square-legs, by taking guard six or eight inches outside the leg stump. On both occasions three balls an over could be left alone with safety as they passed outside the batsman's legs.

An hour had passed, and yet no wicket had fallen—it seemed sufficiently amazing to the watchers in the dressing-room, but quite negatively and unconstructively amazing. Not so, however, to the men in the middle. A faint, a very faint, hope had dawned, and Hobbs waved for a bat. Why, I cannot tell, but I had a hunch that he had something to impart, and so instead of letting the twelfth man (that gallant tyke Maurice Leyland) take the bats out, I took them myself.

"THE BEST INNINGS I EVER PLAYED"

Hobbs cut short my whispered congratulations with the remark, " I want you to come in next." For an awful moment I thought he meant he had been hurt or had pulled a muscle. But no ; he said there was just an outside chance that if we could last the day, without losing too many wickets, we might get the runs on a good wicket next day, and pull a lost match out of the furnace.

It sounded horse-sense, but too good to be true. On returning to the dressing-room, the twelfth man was sent chasing to find Mr. Chapman, while I buckled on my pads " on spec." When the captain came down, he agreed. Another, and for me now, an even more breathless hour passed.

Eventually the first hundred was hoisted, still without the fall of a wicket. Speaking for myself, this was the signal for a wave of confidence ; everything, including the impossible, seemed possible. Almost directly afterwards this bubble was shattered by the fall of Hobbs.

Originally, Hobbs made the start of his outstanding reputation on a sticky wicket at Melbourne in 1908. In the circumstances praise is superfluous or impertinent. It is enough to say that his innings on this occasion after a lapse of twenty years was worthy of that reputation.

VI

Little has been said of Sutcliffe the while, one fears. But that is often the way, for one takes so much for granted with Sutcliffe.

What has been said of Hobbs applies equally to Sutcliffe. On this occasion Hobbs made 49, while Sutcliffe was destined to top the century. He is, *par excellence*, the man for the big effort on the big day, as he proved once again on this occasion. Of my own efforts with the bat the less said the better. Fortunately for any reader who

BAT AND BALL

has read so far, I have mighty few recollections. Suffice it to say that the first two balls I received were well up to me, and I attempted in each case to play them with the deadest of dead bats. Both balls hit me in the solar plexus, but, as the critics said, the wicket had ceased by then to be difficult!

I have a vivid recollection of getting a desperate four through the covers, which helped to disperse the hungry fieldsmen round the bat to Grimmett's bowling. Again an agonising stretch to keep my back foot down, when completely beaten, whilst Oldfield whipped off the bails. . . . However, Sutcliffe remained immovable, and with his example to inspire the pair of us, we survived the day—runs were of little consequence provided wickets did not fall. England were left with nine wickets in hand to get about 160 runs before we were separated on the morrow.

Theoretically it was an easy task on the good wicket of the next day—but one which we very nearly failed to accomplish needlessly and heedlessly.

However, all's well that ends well, it is said, and our cup of joy, already full, was filled to over-brimming by an " impartial " newspaper account, which attributed our win to the luck of having a worn wicket bound together by the rain!

Admittedly Australia had the match cold, and threw it away. Without Hobbs and Sutcliffe, the remaining nine Englishmen could have been bowled out twice on such a wicket for half the runs. One likes to feel that one's best effort, however puny by comparison, went a little way to ensure that the great effort of two giants in a seemingly lost cause had its due reward.

CHAPTER SIX

" The Best Bowling I have ever Done "

BY SIX GREAT BOWLERS

1. HAVOC AMONG THE AUSTRALIANS
    BY WILFRED RHODES

2. ONCE IN A LIFETIME . . .
    BY A. E. R. GILLIGAN

3. LET " WISDEN " TELL THE STORY . . .
    BY A. P. (" TICH ") FREEMAN

4. IN SPITE OF TAKING NO WICKETS . . .
    BY MAURICE TATE

5. ALEXANDER'S FOOTMARKS . . .
    BY HEDLEY VERITY

6. WHY I BOWL LIKE A MAN ASLEEP . . .
    BY W. E. BOWES

CHAPTER SIX

" The Best Bowling I have ever Done "

BY SIX GREAT BOWLERS

HAVOC AMONG THE AUSTRALIANS

BY WILFRED RHODES

MY best bowling? The question is not easy to answer. But I think I ought to choose my performance of nine wickets for 24 runs in the match between C. I. Thornton's XI and the Australians at Scarborough in the summer of 1899. The figures against my name in the score-book were :

O.	M.	R.	W.
18	10	24	9

The wicket was a bit tricky, I confess, but when we consider the number of overs the other bowlers sent down by comparison with mine, not to speak of the strength we were pitted against, more than one wicket might have been expected from them. And because I got so many I can recall no game in which I found greater personal satisfaction—unless it was one at Birmingham in 1902, when I took seven Australian wickets for 17 on behalf of England.

How vividly I remember that Scarborough match after all these years ! Although I was spinning the ball to turn it from leg, while it was in the air it curled towards the batsman from the off. This may have been explained by the fact that the wind was coming from the direction of third man. It sounds a bit of a fairy tale—a ball curving from the off before it pitches and breaking from leg after hitting the ground! But I have often seen it behave like that.

ONCE IN A LIFETIME

BY A. E. R. GILLIGAN

Every moderate fast bowler—to which category I am proud to belong—has a lucky day once in his lifetime, and the Gods of Chance smiled upon me when I captained England against South Africa at Edgbaston in June 1924. Herby Taylor put England in to bat, and we collected 438.

Maurice Tate and I opened the bowling, and I quickly realised that with the week-end dew making its presence felt on the pitch, we had a fast sticky wicket.

My first ball was a wide, but the next sent Bob Catterall's leg stump out of the ground.

Success after success came my way with deliveries which pitched consecutively on the off and leg stumps, and which whipped across at startling speed to scatter them, and sometimes the middle stump as well. In fifty minutes South Africa were out for 30, and I had taken six wickets for 7 runs!

I often wonder nowadays how I achieved this performance, and incidentally many of my friends do as well. It was one of those red-letter days in life's history—pleasant to look back upon in later years—because I believe it is a record.

But, as I said at the start, the Gods of Fortune were on my side that day in June 1924.

"THE BEST BOWLING I HAVE EVER DONE"

LET "WISDEN" TELL THE STORY

BY A. P. ("TICH") FREEMAN

Perhaps it is natural to take a pride in doing at least as well as anybody has ever done, so far as taking lots of wickets for very few runs is concerned. This may be accepted by the reader as the reason why I regard my bowling for Kent against Sussex at Brighton on the last two days of August 1922 as the best of my career.

Let "Wisden" tell the story. "Sussex wound up their season in dismal fashion," he writes in his famous *Cricketers' Almanack*, "Kent beating them by an innings with 23 runs to spare. Beyond everything else the bowling of Freeman stood out by itself. In the whole match he took seventeen wickets for 67 runs—an outstanding performance, much as rain had affected the pitch.

"His nine wickets for 11 runs in the first innings was altogether out of the common even among the many feats of bowlers getting rid of nine or ten men in one innings."

There had been rain with sunshine to follow, as "Wisden" notes, and this made of the pitch the kind which causes the fingers of a spin bowler to burn with anxiety to get going on it.

In the Sussex first innings I seemed to be able to make the ball do anything I wanted it to do, and my analysis was: 10 overs, 4 maidens, 11 runs, 9 wickets. Frank Woolley bagged batsman Number Ten, and the only man to reach double figures was Ted Bowley, who got more than half the runs. There were batsmen in that first innings who were bowled by deliveries which they did not attempt to play, so decided was the spin I was able to give the ball on a pitch that took it readily. In the second innings I had eight wickets for 56 in 23·5 overs.

I have equalled this performance since, but the first

time provides the real thrill, and I still look forward to bagging eighteen victims in a match. Greedy? Well, perhaps; but there's no harm in trying.

IN SPITE OF TAKING NO WICKETS

BY MAURICE TATE

A difficult task, that of deciding about my best bowling performance. So much depends on the point of view. For instance, how can I forget, seeing that I have a silver salver at home to commemorate the feat, the first ball I sent down for England in a Test Match when it got me a wicket and when, in that same first effort, I helped my captain, who was Arthur Gilligan, to dismiss a South African team for 30 in all?

A bowling effort which I shall never forget—because of the special circumstances—was in the game between England and Australia at Adelaide in 1929, which we won by 12 runs. At lunch-time on the last day of the match Australia needed 15 runs to win with two wickets to fall.

England had been in the field for two gruelling days. Oldfield was the one reliable Australian batsman left—the man most likely to knock off the runs. It was my specific task to keep him quiet by bowling so accurately that J. C. White, from the other end, might tempt the less likely run-getters—Oxenham first and then Blackie. Never before, never since, has the demand been made upon me for such a high standard of accuracy in my length. I bowled four successive overs to Oldfield without a run being scored off the bat, four byes being the only addition.

Then, at the other end, Oxenham tried to do just what White intended him to do—to hit a ball to leg. I was fielding there, and I shot out my hand and caught the ball —somehow. Before White's over was ended Blackie had

"THE BEST BOWLING I HAVE EVER DONE"

been caught also, and England won in a thrilling finish by eleven runs.

Four overs, four maidens, no wicket : it doesn't sound impressive as a bowling performance, does it ? All the same, I reckon it one of my best.

If I may mention a wicket-taking performance by way of contrast, I recall without hesitation the 1930 match against the Australians at Nottingham. In less than half an hour, with only 16 runs scored, I had secured the wickets of Ponsford, Woodfull, and Bradman. First I bowled Ponsford round his legs : then I got the Australian captain splendidly caught by A. P. F. Chapman in the gully, and soon afterwards I clean bowled Bradman.

I did not take another wicket in that innings, but if it is granted that pride is ever justifiable, I think I had a right to be proud about this collection of three victims who come high in the list of batsmen most difficult to dislodge.

ALEXANDER'S FOOTMARKS

BY HEDLEY VERITY

It was a day of typical Sydney heat ; it was Sunday afternoon ; I had a comfortable seat on the river bank ; but while my companions, all non-players, read or slept, I could think of nothing but the Test Match we had been playing until the previous evening, and which was to be resumed on the morrow.

Yes, indeed, the legendary Ashes were always my preoccupation. And even here, with nothing to disturb the Sabbath peace, the feeling of joy and of tension, so peculiar to a Test game, persisted. My immediate interest was centred in—footmarks ! . . . the footmarks left by the Australian fast bowler, Alexander, during yesterday's play.

BAT AND BALL

"Think them over, Hedley," our Skipper, D. R. Jardine, had said to me; "they may be useful." And all day his words had been whispering in my mind.

Let me think, I said to myself. There's only one foot-mark that can be used. It is just on the right length, but too far outside the leg stump to offer a match-winning advantage. The "Aussies" are too wily to play at a ball pitched out there. . . . Even if I bowled over the wicket, there'd be only one inch of the rough patch actually on the wicket. Having no long-field out on the on-side might induce them to play at the ball, but I would be left wide open to scoring strokes . . . and Don Bradman would be certain to use his!

Mid-off, mid-on, both deep, three or four short-legs, a deep square-leg, short extra-cover, one slip, and a gully. . . . A spot a foot long, and only three inches wide, even allowing for their errors of judgment. . . . Jove, how accurate I would need to be! . . . Still, it is just possible to bring it off, and it will help Harold Larwood to win us the match if I manage two or three wickets by trying for it.

When I communicated my plan to the Skipper, together with the suggested field, his only comment was: "There seems too much space for these fellows to score runs by means of their off-side strokes." It was an opinion I shared, but it seemed our only chance—and off-side strokes, attempted from deliveries pitched on a rough patch near to the leg-stump might conceivably profit us more than they would the batsman! That is, if I, the bowler, hit the spot.

The match as it stood that week-end was in an even position. We had made 418 for eight in reply to their first-innings total of 438. Monday morning came, and when we were all out we only led by 19 runs, and would have to bat fourth innings. Greeted though he was by

"THE BEST BOWLING I HAVE EVER DONE"

the usual barrage of barrackers, Larwood gave us a splendid start to the Australians' second innings. He dismissed Victor Richardson with his second ball, and 1 for no runs appeared on the score-board. The Sydney fans soon had their drooping spirit revived, however, for Bradman proceeded to make spectacular if risky strokes so fruitfully that 1 for none was changing to 1 for a hundred.

Then our Skipper beckoned me. The testing time for my theory had arrived, and while the crowd were roaring their delight at Don's success I began my attempt to exploit Alexander's footmarks.

The first two balls I bowled to Woodfull hit the spot and turned sharply: and just as sharply a mid-wicket conference was held between the batsmen. Don was down at my end next over, and bang!—four runs came to him through the vacant cover-field. Yet another followed: but then, suddenly he was out—bowled in attempting to repeat the stroke off a delivery that pitched outside the leg stump.

And now Larwood will blaze the trail to another victory, we thought. But, alas! the bowler who had swept through the Australian defences so often had to leave the field with a damaged foot. Well bowled, Harold! His performance had left those of us privileged to watch it amazed at his intense speed and accuracy and full of appreciation of his skill. A broken bone was the price he had to pay, we learnt at the tea interval. And we realised that it was "up to us" to make up for the blow.

That spot on the wicket was no longer a mere help: it had become our main hope. Aided by good fielding it "did us proud." Bill Voce got two quick wickets, and the remaining Australian batsmen fell to balls which I pitched in the roughened soil of those footmarks. The side were all out for 182, and another victory for Jardine and his men seemed assured.

BAT AND BALL

As our opening pair set out on the task of scoring the 164 runs wanted for that victory I thought rather grimly how I had almost discarded my idea of exploiting Alexander's footmarks ! The task of accurately pitching on to a spot a foot long and a few inches wide, and mixing pace at the same time, does not inspire a bowler with rosy dreams. But the Skipper had said " Think it over," and the Skipper had confidence ; and that meant a lot to me when exploiting a half-chance in a Test Match.

WHY I BOWL LIKE A MAN ASLEEP

BY W. E. BOWES

I am somewhat in a position often described as " on the horns of a dilemma." Shall I tell you that my best bowling achievement was one in which I bowled forty overs for 42 runs and no wickets ; or shall I describe to you a feat which requires a certain amount of proof in the way of details to substantiate it ? I have just read in a commentary on the Test Matches between England and Australia in 1934 a criticism of myself, in which the writer wishes to know why fast bowlers walk with that heavy somnambulistic tread—why it is that I bowl like a man with sleep still drowsily soothing my limbs ! Well, I offer no apologies for my actions or inclinations, but possibly the writer I refer to will find a ray of enlightenment in what is to follow.

It was a glorious day in August. Scarborough, that usually bracing Yorkshire resort, was steeped in a stifling heat that made even the holiday-makers and sun-bathers long for the shade, ice-cream, and icy drinks. Yorkshire were playing Essex, and both counties fielded exceptionally strong teams. Essex were anxious to get their revenge

"THE BEST BOWLING I HAVE EVER DONE"

for the first-innings record put up at their expense earlier in the season by Holmes and Sutcliffe, who scored 555 for the first wicket. The ground was packed with a crowd that looked forward to seeing another batting record, or in any case some exceptionally good cricket.

Half an hour before the start of play my colleague Hedley Verity and I went out to inspect the wicket, and I feel sure we both uttered a devout prayer that Yorkshire might win the toss. The wicket was perfect, the heat was intense, and, by way of a little encouragement, the groundsman came up to us with a smile of self-satisfaction and, after enquiring if we didn't think it a good wicket, assured us that if Yorkshire won the toss we could go and hire a deckchair by the sea, and call at the ground next day about lunch-time to see if we were required to bat!

But any hopes we entertained in this direction were very soon dispelled. The Skipper came into our room to inform us that he was very sorry, but he had lost the toss. It was unnecessary to ask who was taking first knock, and Yorkshire took the field with as scanty clothing as possible, and with every bowler hoping against hope that the fates would be kind to us.

Again we were doomed to disappointment, for although Pope and Wilcox were soon out, three slip-catches were dropped off my bowling during my first spell with the new ball. Worse was to follow. It was quickly noticeable that on this beautiful batting wicket the Yorkshire bowlers with less pace than I had were practically innocuous, and the Skipper repeatedly found himself saying: "Sorry, Bill, but it's up to you." Taylor and Nichols played glorious century innings, and it was not until six o'clock that the last wicket fell with the score-board showing 325 runs! I had taken nine at a cost of 121 runs. O'Connor, the one batsman whose wicket I had not captured, had been dropped off my bowling in the slips.

Altogether I had bowled forty overs and one ball, equal to three and a half hours bowling on that terrifically hot day. To say I was tired was putting it mildly, and when, soaked through and through with perspiration, I was informed that a keen Yorkshire supporter had sent in a small bottle of champagne for me—the first I had ever tasted—I was nearly too tired to express my thanks.

My mates were delighted. They wondered how I had managed to stick it in the heat so long—they were not to know that it was they alone who made me force myself, from half-past three until the close of the Essex innings, to run to the wickets and bowl as fast as I could. The reason was this.

I was feeling absolutely finished. The heat was telling on the fieldsmen too—but you will all have heard of the Yorkshire fielding. Taylor drove me towards the boundary in the direction of extra-cover. I scarcely bothered about what happened to the ball, but on looking to see if it had gone for four I was amazed to see third man, gully, and also cover-point racing after it as hard as they could go. The fieldsman who got there first—Arthur Mitchell—beating his two colleagues by a couple of yards, was not satisfied with this; he swung round and flung the ball in as if he intended to run not only one of the batsman out, but all the rest of the Essex team as well!

I shall remember the loyalty of those fieldsmen of ours to the end of my days. I responded, and although I paid the penalty by not sleeping a wink that night or the following night through cramp and the heat, I felt my effort was worth it.

Sutcliffe and Leyland treated the holiday crowd to fireworks next day in reply to the Essex score. Six overs from Farnes, Nichols, and O'Connor brought 102 runs, Sutcliffe actually scoring 75 in four consecutive overs from Farnes! I was excused from batting, and at the

"THE BEST BOWLING I HAVE EVER DONE"

end of the third day Yorkshire had won the match by an innings and 8 runs.

I think of my bowling in that match against Essex not only as my best, but with all due respect to the modesty that becomes a Yorkshireman I recall the result as an excellent victory for an excellent team.

CHAPTER SEVEN

Famous Cricket Grounds

BY J. A. H. CATTON

CHAPTER SEVEN

Famous Cricket Grounds

BY J. A. H. CATTON

> Away they sped with gamesome minds,
>   And souls untouch'd by sin;
> To a level mead they came, and there
>   They drave the wickets in.

THUS Thomas Hood wrote of the happy boys who bounded out of the school at Lynn on an evening prime in summer time when Aram, the usher, sat apart. The contrast—innocence and joy, sin and remorse. Thousands of meadows consecrated to cricket, glistening in silver sunshine and abounding in golden memories, unroll themselves in all parts of the British Isles. Prosaically they are called cricket grounds. Mr. Mark Philips, at one time, nearly a century ago, the millionaire member of Parliament for Manchester, one of the sponsors for launching the Lancashire county club and developing the Old Trafford ground, wrote a letter in 1864 in which he told the committee to put his name down for any sum they thought proper, and he added: " I sincerely wish that every parish in the kingdom possessed a cricket club and a good ground to play upon." In a large measure his desire has been fulfilled. The playing-fields of the schools, the private grounds of gentlemen who relish country-house cricket, the grounds of thousands of clubs, great and small, that are the backbone of cricket, and those large estates that are the headquarters of the counties are found on every hand.

BAT AND BALL

The famous grounds where class matches are played are familiar to devotees all over the world. A public ground may be considered from several points of view : that of the groundsman, who studies the nature of the soil and the length of the roots of the grass ; that of the batsman, the bowler, and the fielder, who each consider the character of the wicket under the influences of the weather ; that of the spectator, who values a clear view, seating, and possibly shelter ; and that of the club and county members, whose demands are similar to those of the average spectator with comforts that exceed the bounds of necessity. These aspects are particular and peculiar. Let us look at some of the grounds with the eyes of the universal man who frequents these rendezvous for an antidote to care, for a rest-place by the highway, and for a protest against the fever of life and the speed that have overtaken the world.

No ground has the prestige of Lord's, the headquarters of Cricket, the home of the Marylebone Club and of Middlesex. This prestige is not wholly derived even from the Marylebone Club, with its unique pre-eminence, history, and achievement. The ground bears the name of Thomas Lord, who took possession in 1813 and laid on the land the turf of the previous pitch of the M.C.C., about half a mile away. The first match recorded on the present Lord's ground was between the M.C.C. and Hertfordshire, with the assistance of H. Bentley, a batsman and afterwards an umpire of renown. Many men of celebrity took part in this game and set a fashion in 1814. The great players for over a century have counted it a day of remembrance when they first appeared at Lord's. The sward deserves to be described as classical if not hallowed ground.

Lord's is known as the Mecca of Cricket. Pilgrims from all parts of the world have worshipped in this shrine of Sport. An Australian team have been known to take off their hats in homage on first passing the gates. This ground is beautiful, and although this may sound heretical, the view from the majestic pavilion when a match is not in progress is truly impressive. Here, near the heart of London, with its throb and animation, is an island of seclusion for the weary and the worried, a solace for the solitary, a refuge from the noise and whirl of wheels, and an amphitheatre for all sorts and conditions of people who relish a pastime free from passion and endowed with peace and the purity of high sport.

The length of Lord's ground is 195 yards, and the width 145 yards, with a fall of seven feet, running from north to south, but so finely graduated that the slope is not apparent at first glance. Beyond this, due east, is another field, about an acre larger, known as the practice ground. This was originally a nursery. A long belt of trees, limes, planes, and chestnuts forms a background to this huge grass-land. At a distance the foliage looks as if it were within Lord's, but these trees are in the churchyard of St. John, Marylebone, with its grey cupola; and still farther beyond are the miniature minarets and decorative scroll chimneys of lofty residences. The prospect is picturesque. The circle devoted to match play is surrounded by stands. There was a time when an ivy-clad tennis court stood on the south side, but this was dismantled and the Mound Stand reared on the site. On the north a new grandstand was built and brought into use in 1926. From this a balcony, in enamel white, has been ingeniously carried round about one-third of the arena until joining the Mound Stand. Under the eaves of the balcony are seats for those who prefer shade for the eyes.

Lord's, with its modern equipment for the need of momentous matches, has not lost in attraction by the gain in utility. The Marylebone Club has a wonderful estate, an island of property of the estimated value of £2,000,000.

With a considerable staff the year round, the expenditure upon maintenance amounts to £12,000 a year. No other club has an establishment of such magnitude.

On the southern side of the Thames, and in the parish of Kennington, is The Oval, known everywhere as the ground of the Surrey Club. In 1844 the Montpelier, a South London Club, were in danger of losing their ground, but they heard that an oval-shaped market garden, situated behind the Kennington Tavern, and belonging to the Duchy of Cornwall, was likely to become vacant. The Montpelier secured a lease of the land for the game. This site was laid out for cricket by turfing three acres and a half. A Surrey Club was established and began to play on the new ground, the first match being against the M.C.C. in May 1846. Troubles arose, and in 1851 the solicitor to the Duchy brought a Bill to Parliament to build two crescents on the oval, but the Prince Consort, managing the estate for the young Prince of Wales, declared that The Oval should be available for cricket so long as the people of South London wished. Eventually Surrey leased the ground and the wicket became famous for the purposes of the batsman. In no sense can The Oval be termed attractive apart from the matches played there, but as a very large open stretch of grass-land in the midst of a congeries of streets and near immense gasometers the ground may be considered as a reservoir of fresher air than would otherwise have been possible had houses been built.

In one way Lancashire's ground at Manchester is similar to Lord's owing to the spacious practice ground adjoining the circle set aside for match play. It is doubtful if any clubs, save the M.C.C. and the Lancashire, have two grounds large enough for the playing of any match, although, of course, there is only accommodation for sightseers on one of them. The Old Trafford match ground was originally two fields on a farm and was made into a cricket pitch in 1857 by the removal of a thorn hedge which divided them. Although this growth was uprooted, there remained a distinct line in the middle of the grass for more than half a century. The first big match was played there in 1859, and the first inter-county game between Lancashire and Middlesex in July 1865. The estate, which originally belonged to the De Trafford family, is a monument to the enthusiasm of the old cricketers of the county, for the Manchester Club was founded in the days of Napoleon. Players agree that as an open space with rare turf, jealously protected and carefully tended, swept by every wind and blessed with an abundance of light, Old Trafford is unsurpassed in England. The surroundings are flat and uninteresting, but fine scenery is not a necessity for good cricket.

The Liverpool Club has a really pretty ground at Aigburth. Trees abound on all sides, but not in such positions as to interfere with perfect sight of the ball, or so tall as to influence light. Every kind of tree has charms, but these are not an advantage on a cricket field save in the form of a piece of willow, perfect in grain and substance, or a shapely stick of ash, ready to be felled again. Aigburth has a sylvan setting, with a stretch of lawn where ladies in wicker-chairs take tea. Just below the gables of the pavilion roof there is a verandah giving a view of the mountain tops of Wales. Truly Aigburth is a pleasant place.

The Yorkshire Club have not a ground that is their own property. Bramall Lane, Sheffield, used rightly to be regarded as the headquarters. One says rightly, because Sheffield played so big a part in founding the Yorkshire County Club. Years ago the offices were removed to Leeds and the Headingley ground became their " home." The team are " at home " anywhere within the borders of some three million acres. The Bramall Lane ground was laid out before there was a county club, by the Sheffield United Club, who secured a field in the middle of the city, on a lease for sixty years, from the Duke of Norfolk. This land was set apart for cricket, archery, and kindred sports by gentlemen who each subscribed £5, and became known as the proprietors. The first match at cricket was played on April 30th and May 1st, 1855, whereas the Y.C.C.C. was not established until 1862, although games of historic interest were played near Sheffield early in the century.

The ground, surrounded by mean streets and tall chimneys, became a lung in an industrial quarter and the resort of workers, who regarded this scene for sport as a foretaste of paradise. Fred Grace, the youngest of the Graces of cricket, said that he would sooner field on the boundary there than anywhere in England, as he revelled in the original comments of the Sheffield grinders, who were a racy, if not a Rabelaisian, folk. Headingley offered a vivid contrast, for the ground was in the midst of villadom with " desirable residences," and suggestions of woodlands, and that within hail of a commercial centre. From Scarborough to Sheffield, from Hull to Huddersfield, the cricket net is spread, but it is doubtful if any one of the grounds is entrancing because of environment. They serve their purpose, and in another sense are beauty-spots, for the Yorkshire eleven " paint the meadows with delight " wherever they pitch and toss.

The famous Trent Bridge ground at Nottingham was laid out by William Clarke, the founder of the " All England Eleven "—merely a myth to this generation. Clarke was described to the writer by George Parr in these terms : " Excepting his own faults, Clarke knew more than any man about cricket." At least he was sufficiently worldly-wise to marry a widow who was the hostess of a quaint and comfortable old-fashioned inn, with a thatched roof, situated on the south side of the bridge spanning the Trent with many small arches. This little house, belonging to the Chaworth-Musters family, had a large field. Clarke foresaw the possibility of the game being played on an enclosed ground, instead of on the vast meadows, open and free to all. Therefore Clarke laid down a wicket, fenced in the field, and charged admission. To the lacemakers the change was not popular.

The ground was used in 1839 and the first county match played there in 1840. Trent Bridge ground, which eventually became the property of the Notts County Club, was a fine arena before being encircled with stands. Fifty years ago there was just a great grass plot with a picturesque pavilion of wood and glass, somewhat in the manner of a mammoth greenhouse, though with a flat roof. Apart from members, spectators sat on long wooden forms more suitable for a schoolroom than a cricket ground. A waiter, in the middle of a hoop, with cans of home-brewed ale suspended from it, walked about looking for customers. Some cronies used to gather near to " George Parr's tree," for Parr, a celebrated batsman, was wont to hit over the tree with frequent strokes to leg. When Parr passed away, a branch from this fine elm, still standing, was placed on the coffin and over his grave. " The Bridges," as the ground was called by the natives, has pleasant vistas, but, like Headingley, has been built in. Yet with over ninety years of cricket on this pasture-land, one forgets even the Trent, with the woods of Colwick, and the villages on its banks that have produced players of renown.

Neighbours of Notts, the counties of Leicestershire and Derbyshire, fell under the spell of cricket. In ancient days the game was played in such rich and rural surroundings as at Loughborough, with Beacon Hill and Charnwood Forest offering a wonderful background, and once upon a time in the midst of such lovely landscape as

Chatsworth offers. As the game moved southwards in these counties there were no such surroundings. In Warwickshire cricket was played in such interesting places as Leamington, Coventry, and Rugby, until the idea of centralising at Birmingham occurred. The Warwickshire Club obtained twelve acres of meadow-land belonging to Lord Calthorpe. This plot, situated between Calthorpe Park and Cannon Hill Park, was not only quite pleasant, but was coated with excellent turf. The new ground, in the suburb of Edgbaston, was opened in June 1885, with a match between Warwickshire and the M.C.C. The trees of the parks reminded the visitors that they were in leafy Warwickshire and near the forest of Arden. The wood-built pavilion is sufficiently antique to recall the Trent Bridge structure prior to 1886.

Kent's principal ground, known as the St. Lawrence, is at Canterbury. This field never looks so entrancing as during the August festival, the parent of the " weeks " at Tonbridge, Tunbridge Wells, Folkestone, Maidstone, and Dover. The social side of Kent cricket possesses some of the carnival spirit of the Continent, for each town is gay with bunting, illuminations, and entertainment. Nevertheless, St. Lawrence has the atmosphere of old times and the countryside. Marquees and tents, decorated and bright with flowers, are near the boundaries, with trees towering behind them. At the Lexington end, opposite the old-fashioned pavilion, a mass of colour, the gold-tinted brown of a corn-field, ripely swaying in the breeze, seems to emphasise a fancy that cricket has been transplanted in the big towns. It was indigenous to pastures adjoining the arable lands. " Cannerberry " cricket presents many pictures, but nothing so alluring as this corn-field. Tonbridge is not quite so rural, nor Tunbridge Wells, with all its woodlands, quite so ravishing. The Mote Park, Maidstone, with its " tall ancestral trees " is captivating, but cricketers have no more appreciation of foliage than the foxhunters of violets in bloom. Folkestone, so huge that it was said that no batsmen could hit " a six," is a delight. Still the boundaries have been carried by the long driver. Of arenas bordering the shores of Kent, the Crabble ground at Dover, perched on a hill, claims attention, for here is a space that could be made to accommodate the greatest crowd that ever watched a Test Match. This ground, almost the centre of a natural amphitheatre, affords a view of Dover Castle which does not seem much higher above the sea-level. Swelling downs unfold behind a country residence converted into a pavilion. Lovers of cricket who dwell in Kent are fortunate.

The county ground of Sussex at Hove is renowned for its fertility of runs, but as a camera scene cannot compare with Horsham's ground, approached by an avenue of enchantment, or with Eastbourne-by-the-Downs and the Mayor's parlour window, giving His Worship a free view of the game. Eastbourne, with its trees on one side and the Downs on the other, is much praised even by the most practical of batsmen who consider the possibilities of the pitch before everything. Hastings, with its modest appointments, but with hundreds, aye, almost thousands, of chairs, suggests a garden party in the grounds of the old castle on the hill.

Within the borders of Hampshire is Broad-Halfpenny, the far-famed field of the old Hambledon Club—probably the only cricket club that has ever inspired literature. The Hambledon worthies were not as other men and other cricketers. They stand alone as much as the royal waxworks in Westminster Abbey. Still, even Broad-Halfpenny, with memories antique, and the hallowed ground of those enthusiasts who worship the cradle of cricket, is not within the scope of this review. The spirit of sport at Hambledon survived the club. Southampton seems to have had a ground before the recollections of the oldest inhabitant. For instance, there was the Antelope ground, laid out by a cricketer, on land belonging to the living of St. Mary's Church. The Ecclesiastical Commissioners felt compelled to sell this plot to the builders. In 1884 steps were taken to get a ground for the county. Eight acres at Bannister Park, the property of Sir Edward Hulse, Bart., were obtained and equipped through the foresight and perseverance of Colonel Fellowes, R.E. Bannister Park appeals as a beautiful home of sport.

After many vicissitudes Ashley Down at Bristol has become definitely the utilitarian headquarters of Gloucestershire, though the club play matches on far more favoured spots without going to such a remote corner of the county as Moreton-in-the-Marsh. It is difficult to imagine county contests being taken to Moreton, even though it is in the area of the Cotswolds. Somerset, like Gloucestershire and Hampshire, have their own principal ground at Taunton. This property originally belonged to Major Winter, of Watts House, Taunton. Comparatively, this is a little ground, hard by the church and the River Tone, and has become renowned as a spot beloved by batsmen who revel in the sound of a smite for six. Still there is the beauty of Bath with "its abbey dear" and its downs so famed. The Worcester ground has lost some of its arresting features, but runs in plenty can still be made on the banks of the Severn with the cathedral pile on the other side of the river.

At last Essex have abandoned the prosaic ground at Leyton, eleven acres and more in extent, that were bought from Lord Cobham for £12,000, in 1885. The experiment of leaving Brentwood, so as to be near to the east of London, has not been the success expected, and the Essex eleven have been driven to wandering about the east

FAMOUS CRICKET GROUNDS

of the county to such places of attraction as Colchester, Chelmsford, and Southend. During the twentieth century several county clubs have been compelled to realise that one central ground for a whole county is not convenient for all. Cricket has to be taken to the people. The use of many grounds, never designed for county cricket, has become necessary. Some of them have pleasant aspects. Others certainly have a feeling of rusticity that one likes to associate with a game that was born and nursed on village greens and pastoral plains. Leyton was foreign to such a feeling. Leyton is not to be blamed, for Leyton had no say in the matter. The Essex Club chose to go to Leyton. Now they are cultivating fresh fields. At least one of them, once more in rural Brentwood, is among the loveliest in the land.

Cricket has been a vogue at the ancient seats of learning for more than a hundred years. At Cambridge the game was played on Parker's Piece until F. P. Fenner, an excellent player, became a tenant of Caius College and, under the patronage of the Earl of Stamford and Lord Burghley, opened a ground in 1846. Two years afterwards the University began to play at " Fenner's." The University obtained possession in 1873, bought the freehold in 1892, and desired the world to abandon the phrase " at Fenner's " and adopt the title of the Cambridge University Cricket Ground. This retreat is worthy of a formal title, for it is secluded and agreeable ; a place with a perfect lawn on which a fine wicket could anywhere be set up. Oxford University had the use of the ground of the old Bullingdon Club, and also of the college grounds of Magdalen and Christ Church. About 1881 the colleges were left to enjoy their own recreation fields, as the University secured ten acres in the Parks for the purpose of matches and practice. This ground, in the middle of the Parks, with a belt of trees, copper-beeches among the verdure, is serene and beautiful. The trees may appeal more to the spectator than to the player, who finds that the ball can so frequently be " lost in the trees." And when unfavourable weather forbids cricket either at Cambridge or Oxford, spend a little time in the pavilions, for on the walls, inscribed in rich lettering, are the names of the captains. This is the honours list of university cricket.

CHAPTER EIGHT
Test-match Cricket
BY JACK HOBBS

CHAPTER EIGHT

Test-match Cricket

BY JACK HOBBS

TEST cricket is something to be thankful for—from one point of view ; and something to be sorry about —from another. There can be no two opinions as to its peculiar distinction, however ; it stands apart from every other kind of cricket, and the fiercest struggle for the county championship fails to impose itself on the mind as Test Matches do, even when they are outside those played between England and Australia. Certainly there is nothing in ordinary cricket to be compared with the excitement of an Anglo-Australian encounter. Of course, the series of Tests between England and the West Indies, India, New Zealand, or even South Africa, have not, so far, set the cricketing continents on tip-toe, but the glamour is there all the same.

And what glamour ! Here in England the eager throng pours into Nottingham, Manchester, Leeds, or London, and packs round the arena as it seldom or never does at an inter-county match. Rich men, poor men . . . everybody is cricket mad, mad for an English victory. And yonder in Australia the sheep-farmers, merchants, stockriders, pour into Sydney, Melbourne, Adelaide, Brisbane—rich men, poor men—even more cricket mad for an Australian victory. Many of them travel a thousand miles under the blazing southern skies just to see their team beat ours !—although, when I come to think of it, a thousand miles is only a big effort in a relative sense, for hundreds of the elect travel all the way to

England to watch the fortunes of their champions over here.

The atmosphere of Test cricket resembles that of the club and county game in a noteworthy sense, though. For better or worse, big cricket in all its branches has altered since the Great War. The old sparkle seems to have gone out of it. We are not so light-hearted in our comings and our goings. The commercial side has been developed, and consequently cricket is more competitive, played less for its own sake, and in many aspects keener and grimmer. My purpose in this chapter is not to seek and find the reason why. I will restrict myself to making a brief quotation from my book *Playing for England*, in which I draw a line between the Test Matches that were played before 1914–18 and those which have followed after; a heavy black line that marks the end of one epoch and the beginning of another:

" I cannot help thinking that the decline of amateurism has been a big factor. Economic conditions in the workaday world have deprived the unpaid player of the necessary leisure, so that professionalism is not sufficiently leavened. Hence the talk about 'speeding up' cricket to meet the demands of a new civilisation, and all that sort of thing, has been treated more seriously than it would be if there were more independent players."

It is, I think, this change in the atmosphere that led Mr. D. R. Jardine, a Test-match captain in post-war cricket, to declare that although to approach a Test Match as " second only to the Battle of Waterloo " may not be the ideal thing, it has much to recommend it. " A Test Match, one feels, is the real thing, with the gloves off while it lasts."

In many respects Test cricket remains the same. Its settings have merely been added to—by the raising of India, the West Indies, and New Zealand to full status. The ancient battle-fields have remained. In Australia, the home of Victor Trumper, Charles Macartney, Don Bradman, there is The Oval at Sydney, the best ground in the world from the player's standpoint, with its perfect light and open skies behind the bowler's arm at both ends; Melbourne, the world's best-equipped arena, that mostly remains the same old place I first knew, with the same old dressing-room and its little windows, the only change being outside, notably a marvellous score-board and a grand pavilion that cost £90,000; Adelaide, of the trees, the cathedral, and hills in the distance; and Brisbane, a workmanlike ground that only requires a little improvement to make it worthy of Titanic battles. Nor is there much that has altered at the centres of Test cricket in South Africa, that sun-sweet homeland of Aubrey Faulkner, Dave Nourse, and "Herby" Taylor. There is the pretty, tree-encircled Capetown ground at Newlands, with the blue Table Mountain, white cloud-tipped, in the shimmering distance; the old ground at Durban, pleasant with green, semi-tropical leafage and green grass; and the Jo'burg ground, where until lately there was not a blade of grass to be seen. Here there is still Trent Bridge, Nottingham, hallowed by countless memories, a pleasant place yet, though practically surrounded in these days by grandstands; Birmingham, hardly ever used now for Test Matches, but with the quaint, rustic air about it as of old; Old Trafford, also a home of memories, our best ground so far as light is concerned, because the sight is not overshadowed at either end; Leeds, that will always be associated in my mind with that splendid manager of cricket tours, Sir Frederick Toone, who did not live long, alas! to enjoy his knighthood; Lord's, the magnificent; and finally, Kennington Oval, a terribly difficult ground on which to see the ball against the pavilion when you are batting, and against the houses and gasometers when you are fielding.

Test cricket has not changed in other ways, either. It is still possible for us to experience the thrill of great batting and bowling, and the close finish. I can recall several grand climaxes in my own career as a Test player, but I think those of longer experience would claim that the two Anglo-Australian Tests at Manchester and Kennington Oval in 1902, when, respectively, Australia won by 3 runs and England by one wicket, are unique as narrow victories and defeats. For my own part I still recall with a quickening of the pulse my first Test Match as one that had the most thrilling finish I have ever known in International cricket. It was at Melbourne in 1907-8, and England wanted 282 to win in their fourth innings. When our eighth wicket fell we were 73 behind and it seemed as if defeat was again to be ours. But one of the transformations came at that point for which cricket will always be glorious. Humphries and Barnes stayed together until we wanted 39. We hardly dared hope that these runs would be got by Barnes and Fielder, who were both in the side for their bowling. And yet ... had not Hazlitt and Cotter knocked off the 56 that Australia needed in the first Test, and were not Hazlitt and Cotter played for *their* bowling? Anyway, Barnes and Fielder stuck it gallantly: the total crept up and up, until the score-board read 281 for 9. This brought the scores dead level and our two bowler-batsmen were still together! I have told the rest of the story elsewhere in these words:

" 'Don't you move!' So, to one another, whispered the rest of us as we looked out from the dressing-room. The tension had become almost overwhelming; and there we stood, crowding, half-dressed, at the windows with socks or shoes in our hands, not daring to move a muscle lest we changed the luck of the two batsmen out on the field! Cricketers are very superstitious in some ways! If things are going all right there is great anxiety that everybody should sit tight and keep their places. If they don't . . . !

" . . . Sid Barnes faced the bowling. He had a death-or-glory expression on that keen face of his. He and Fielder were so excited that they decided to run wherever the ball went, Barnes hit it towards cover—only a few yards, but they ran for all they were worth.

" If Jerry Hazlitt, the fieldsman, had thrown straight, there might have been a different finish to tell about; but Hazlitt, too, was excited, and he threw the ball wildly, so wide of the stumps and the stumper that three Australians tried one after another to stop it and failed as it flew to the boundary!

" When that winning hit was completed Fielder ran on and on for sheer joy and didn't slow down until he was half-way to the pavilion. What a reception awaited him and Sid Barnes from the sporting Melbourne crowd—especially Barnes. I was having my first experience of this wonderful all-rounder. I did not know many of the team very well, and I had never met Barnes until we met on the journey from England. He did not then belong to any county : he was playing in League cricket, and A. C. Maclaren had made a sensational discovery of him. If Maclaren's 'cricket-sense' ever wants vindication—which it won't—he need only point to Barnes, the very best bowler I have ever seen."

Many Test Matches in which I have figured since that Melbourne thriller become vivid in my memory as I look back, either for their drama, their breath-taking climax, or their magnificence. One of the most magnificent I have ever taken part in, one of the most magnificent in all the history of cricket, was that which England won at The Oval in 1926. Australia led on the first innings by 302 to 280, and Herbert Sutcliffe and I began England's second venture an hour before the close of Monday's play. A critical time to go in, but we kept together. During the night there was a heavy thunderstorm, and although the wicket was fairly easy to begin with the next morning, it gradually became more difficult. I thought we had precious little chance. The "Aussies" had a wicked glint in their eyes, and they were on tip-toe. I guessed that the great crowd felt what I was feeling, for I heard their sigh of relief at the end of each over, especially those of them who sat on the pavilion and looked down-wicket, for they could see Arthur Richardson turning the ball and knew why he had three or four short-legs.

At one period Richardson bowled so well that I just couldn't get away from his end. But Sutcliffe and I managed to keep together, and at lunch-time we were 161 for none. I was 97 and he was 63. We felt we had pulled the game round, and so we had. After lunch I completed my hundred and a few minutes later a fine ball from Gregory took my off-bail. We were 172 then, and Herbert Sutcliffe continued, superbly, dominatingly, flawlessly, until the last ball of the day, when he was bowled by Mailey. He had scored 161, and at the close that Tuesday night we were 375 for six, or 353 ahead with four wickets standing.

With the possible exception of the occasion on which I scored three centuries in consecutive Tests in Australia, I cannot remember being so exhilarated as I was that night. I had done my bit; I knew the wicket was badly knocked about, and that we were in an almost impregnable position. When our innings ended next day we gave Australia 415 to win—and now came Wilfred Rhodes's great moment. Rhodes, who played his first Test Match against Australia twenty-seven years earlier, had to be persuaded into this one, his forty-first. He felt himself too old, too stiff, and he couldn't bowl, he couldn't bat, he couldn't field ! But his fellow-selectors—for he and I had been co-opted on to the Committee—listened to none of his arguments, and that closing day he took the wickets of Bardsley, Ponsford, Collins, and Richardson !

This was the first and only time I have ever seen the old enemy throw in their hand. They did absolutely give up. And the end came soon after six o'clock with only 125 runs on the score-board, and we had won by 289 runs. The scene that came next was, to me, an essential part of Test cricket. The delirious crowd bore down on us, and we raced off at top speed towards the pavilion. I was cut off, and had to be protected by policemen. A huge black mass, cheering, yelling, waving their hats, packed the space in front of the pavilion, and demanded player after player.

Well, the Australian crowds have had reason to be just as hero-worshipping, ecstatic. The destiny of the Ashes has been a see-saw affair—first one side winning, then the other, except when a prolonged bad patch has been struck —as it was with England immediately after the Great War. It will be found that the touring side has in a large number of instances won the rubber. That is because they are more of a team, suffering fewer changes than the home side. Also they are single-minded; their attention is not diverted all summer from their one big purpose. Since the tournament began—in 1876, although a cricket team set sail from England to Australia in a paddle steamer fifteen years earlier—we have won 32 matches " down under," which is only fewer by 6 than our defeats; over here, where, the matches being mostly limited in time, there have been 27 drawn, we have won only 20 to the Australians' 15.

Great names have starred the long history of Test cricket, and will, of course, continue to do so. Steel, Spofforth, Giffen, Grace, and Lyttleton; Bonnor, Shrewsbury, Turner, Ferris, and Stoddart; C. B. Fry, Ranjitsinhji, J. T. Brown, Albert Ward, Barnes, Ernest Jones, and Tom Richardson ; Noble and Hill ; Maclaren, Trumper, Darling, Trumble, Woolley, Gregory, and Macdonald ; Warner, Jackson, Gunn, Macartney, Rhodes, Maurice Tate, Mailey, Hammond, Grimmett, Sutcliffe, Larwood, and Bradman ; Gilligan, Chapman, Jardine, Hendren—the names go on and on. . . . The South African sky has flashed with some of them : Herbert Taylor and Dave Nourse ; Aubrey Faulkner, Schwarz, Vogler, and White—what bowlers, these four ! Constantine and Headley of the West Indies are already among the immortals. The Anglo-Australian struggle has been guided, moreover, by some great captains. I have played under or against half a dozen of them : Warwick Armstrong, Archie Maclaren, P. F. Warner, P. G. H. Fender, A. O. Jones, and M. A. Noble. Fender was the best I have played under : but I regard "Monty" Noble as the greatest of them all.

Once upon a time our overseas rivals included Philadelphia. To-day we find five countries—Australia, South Africa, West Indies, India, and New Zealand—with Test-match status. This extension is proof of the increasing popularity of International cricket, and ever greater becomes the honour of wearing the England cap with the three silver lions !

CHAPTER NINE
Cricket Tours Abroad
BY A. P. F. CHAPMAN

CHAPTER NINE

Cricket Tours Abroad

BY A. P. F. CHAPMAN

WHAT *is* " abroad " ? There appears to be some difference of opinion as to where to draw the line. For if we consider the well-known quotation—

Whene'er I take my walks abroad—

the word obviously means anywhere outside the garden gate and within " hiking " distance, but limited to the coasts of Great Britain. On the other hand, a friend of mine, on drawing a little extra cash from the bank for a trip to Germany, told the cashier that he was going *abroad*. " Oh ! " said the latter, after enquiring about the destination, " that's only *on the Continent* ; I thought you said you were going abroad ! "

And so I feel that I may fairly claim a considerable amount of licence, though personally I should include all countries outside the British Isles as being " abroad." As a matter of fact, one feels more at home in Australia or New Zealand, in spite of the distance, than one does in Calais or Boulogne.

Tours abroad, for all kinds of sport, have multiplied exceedingly in the last few years. In fact, there is hardly a country in the world which does not compete with us nowadays in some game or other. And, conversely, there is hardly any form of sport—whether it be on land or water or air, mounted or afoot or awheel, active or sedentary, indoors or out-of-doors—in which we do not compete with representatives from overseas. Of course, there are the

BAT AND BALL

Olympic Games to start with; but for special forms of sport, look at Bisley, Henley, Brooklands, Wimbledon, St. Andrews, etc., and mark the number of countries represented. And for most of these countries representative teams leave our shores in return, chiefly for cricket, football, lawn tennis, golf, and athletics. What a change in the standard of play this competition (which in itself owes its cause to facility of transport) has brought about in all countries, including our own!

It is very difficult for us players of the present day to realise that, not much more than a century ago, the only means of land transport was horseflesh, and that the games themselves, as we know them, only began to exist more recently still. A hundred years seems a long time, but, after all, it is but a very small fraction of the history of the world. Railways and round-arm bowling came in practically together—only under-hand bowling was allowed up till then—and as over-arm bowling was only made legal in 1865, cricket, as we know it, is not more than seventy years old at present. But cricket tours abroad had already begun, for it was in 1862 that an exhibition side visited Australia, playing against teams of eighteen and twenty-two.

It is interesting to note, in passing, the progress of other games during the same period. Football, which had been a rough-and-tumble sort of game (vide *Tom Brown's Schooldays*), was becoming organised, and taken up by schools and universities; but it was not until 1863 that the Football Association was formed. The Rugby Union followed in 1871. Golf (except, of course, at Blackheath and a few other places) was unknown in England until about 1870; and as for lawn tennis, it was not even invented until somewhere around 1877.

The advent of the railways, therefore, set things moving in more senses than one. Towards the end of the cen-

CRICKET TOURS ABROAD

tury, tours, both at home and abroad, were organised in all directions. " All England " teams toured this country, consisting of some of the first-class players of the day (including W. G. Grace himself) and showing cricketers in out-of-the-way places a standard of play which they would otherwise have had but little chance of seeing. There was hardly a club of any standing, whether it had a home ground of its own or not, which did not run a tour of some sort. One could hardly enter any large station, especially during the holiday month of August, without seeing on the platform a barrow or two piled up with cricket bags (several of them probably gaping open and showing well-known colours). Seaside places on the whole offered the greatest attraction, but it was no uncommon sight to see, at wayside country stations, a smart brake with a pair of smart horses, and a pony-cart, waiting to convey the tourists and their luggage to some well-kept country-house ground in the neighbourhood.

But the war put a stop to all that. Every cricketer over eighteen years of age joined up, and a vast proportion of them were either killed or disabled : cricket grounds (except at schools) were deserted ; and even Lord's became a training-ground for soldiers, and creepers overgrew the faces of the clocks there. So cricket had to make a fresh start in 1919 under considerably changed conditions, which we find, after numerous years of peace, have materially affected tours at home more than those abroad.

First of all, there is the shortage of money, for a tour of any kind is bound to be more or less expensive, and somebody has to pay. Touring teams (unless representative) are usually composed entirely of amateurs, and your amateur of to-day can rarely command the time and money for such luxuries : he has to think of his career and work for his living. And besides, now that country-house cricket is a rarity and so many of the big places, where both teams were entertained, are turned into orphanages or girls' schools, he probably has to pay every penny of his travelling, hotel, and refreshment expenses himself, not to mention his quota for the umpire and scorer.

Secondly, there is the motor-car, which has altered the methods of life of the whole world, and cricket tours amongst them. Very few people travel by train nowadays if they can help it: travelling by train has gone out of fashion. What cricketer wants to go on a tour when he can chuck his things, any old how, into a car, play a match within a radius of fifty or sixty miles, and get home again the same evening? He can get as much cricket as ever he wants that way, and be at the office next morning. Probably, before long, the aeroplane will come into use and we shall see an England team starting for Australia by air-liner!

Thus far I have commented on the rise and fall of cricket tours in general, but henceforward I must confine myself to my original subject—namely, cricket tours abroad. It has always been a source of wonderment to me that such a splendid game as cricket has never caught on in European countries to any great extent, though it appears to be becoming fairly well rooted in Holland. Other ball-games are played, and most successfully (as we well know), and why not cricket? I suppose it is chiefly due to temperament and tradition. So far as Holland is concerned, though I personally have never been on tour there, I can imagine that grounds can be obtained without much expense in levelling, and I hear that the tours there are most enjoyable.

And tours are *meant* to be enjoyable. Cricket, after all, is a game; and a game is intended to be played for the fun of the thing, though there is no fun in any game unless you are keen to win it. You may get a lot of fun *while*

CRICKET TOURS ABROAD

playing any game, but you get it in other ways, and not out of the game itself. Keenness there must be, and you strive with all your power—body, soul, and spirit—to help your side to win. But there is such a thing as *over*-keenness, which tends to produce envy, hatred, malice, and all uncharitableness, and, if any of these ugly things appear, bang goes all chance of enjoyment. Our matches in Australia (where the atmosphere seems charged with electricity, and where the cries of the excited crowds of spectators are liable to upset the equilibrium of the players) have suffered a good deal from this over-keenness lately. Can it be possible, seeing that players seem to get more excited when there is something tangible in view, that that insignificant little urn can have made any difference?

No doubt there are players who are blessed with such a temperament that they can truthfully say that they really *enjoyed* the actual play in a Test Match abroad, but they must be very few : in most cases, if not all, the nervous tension crowds out the enjoyment. In this respect, therefore, the tour of the Test team suffers by comparison with that of a non-representative side, which is run entirely for enjoyment, though possibly there may be a pioneering purpose in it as well.

In the latter case Mr. Blank, a well-known and enthusiastic cricketer, is invited, or offers, to take a team out to Ruritania, and at once proceeds to collect a side, strong enough for the purpose, as far as possible from among his own personal friends and acquaintances. I use the word " collect " advisedly : for to " select " a side is a very different matter, as every secretary knows. Of course he invites the best cricketers he can, but at the same time keeps a corner of his eye widely open for goodfellowship. " Tour will last about six weeks ; cricket not too strenuous ; not much travelling ; good wickets, excellent climate, and lovely scenery ; splendid golf and bathing; expense will only be about umpty pounds, as we get put up most of the time: Bill Smith and Jack Robinson are going; do come." And so in due time a jovial party, probably consisting of public-school and university men, assembles at Southampton, well equipped with golf-clubs and tennis-rackets, and sets out without much public attention. In the press next day one may read, " A cricket team sailed yesterday by the s.s. *Saxonia* for a six-weeks' tour in Ruritania under the management and captaincy of Mr. R. C. Blank," and that's about all. A bit later on one may see the scores published, without much comment. The matches have been interesting and most of them won, if not all; and the team comes peacefully home again, having seen a lot of country, thoroughly enjoyed itself (though a bit out of pocket), and leaving behind a host of new friends and a good impression.

But the representative team is under the public eye from start to finish, and for six months leads a strenuous life. Leaving out the strain of the cricket, the enjoyment of the varied experiences of the tour depends upon the tastes of the individual. For example, some people thoroughly enjoy a long sea voyage; others are frankly bored with it, even if (and first-class cricketers are but human) they do not suffer from sea-sickness. On board of a big ocean liner of twenty thousand tons or more, one *may* be lucky enough to travel the whole way from England on an even keel, but there is usually a bit of a roll, more or less pronounced, to which the worst sailor soon gets accustomed. But on smaller boats (as, for instance, while crossing from Australia to Tasmania) even the most hardy mariner will probably find himself fairly tested. One voyage is very much like another, but the presence of a party of athletic and high-spirited young cricketers more than doubles the fun of all the deck games, dances, etc., which are run on every ship. Of course they carry off amongst them nearly all the prizes in competitions such as quoits and tennis, but it does not necessarily follow that they can beat the ship's company in deck cricket. Sometimes the latter can turn out quite a hot side at this peculiar form of the game. Perhaps they are more accustomed to the surroundings ; the motion of the ship ; the dazzling light ; and the presence of a chattering crowd of spectators six feet behind the bowler's arm ! Or perhaps they take the game a trifle more seriously ! A cricket ground ninety feet long, twelve feet wide, and eight feet high forms rather a contrast to Trent Bridge or The Oval, and the setting of the field does not present much room for ingenuity : silly-point, silly-cover-point, silly-everything ! However, this is the only form of cricket which one gets on the way out except (in the case of an Australian tour) at Colombo, where a match is so arranged with a Ceylon side that the locals may always see the tourists bat for a good part of the time. If you want a taste of unadulterated heat, try a cricket match at Colombo in October, for the atmosphere is usually like a Turkish bath, and you will need your towel. A stiff collar and a boiled shirt have been a practical impossibility ever since Port Said, but the match at Colombo takes the starch out of your body as well. However, you are royally entertained and the whole experience is delightful.

Next comes Perth, and the really strenuous time begins, about which one cannot write in detail without filling a volume, and concerning the cricket part of which many books are published. The strain is not so great in countries other than Australia, for the sense of rivalry is not so intense, but the experiences remain the same in varying degree. Crowds on arrival ; crowds on departure ; crowds at wayside stations : crowds at public functions and civic receptions ; crowds at race-courses ; crowds at matches. Photographers, autograph hunters, and pressmen everywhere ; and be careful what you say, or some innocent but unguarded remark " may be used as evidence against you." Invitations to dinners, dances, theatres, concerts, mines, farms, and factories; some of them difficult to refuse without giving offence. Boating, bathing, golf, tennis, and fishing on off days. Dust and insects; a broiling sun overhead; cricket-grounds of iron, and sometimes mud or matting. Packing and unpacking; hundreds of miles of travelling by road or rail, sometimes through lovely scenery and sometimes over dreary wastes, but nearly always with something novel to see. Buildings, gardens, caves, mountains, waterfalls, and geysers; natives and their villages; unfamiliar types of animals, birds, and reptiles.

From a sight-seeing point of view, I should say that South Africa is the most interesting of those countries which I personally have toured. Not only does each province present its own special type of scenery, colouring, inhabitants, and products, but it has more historical interest as well. As for delicious fruits and gorgeous sub-tropical flowers, they abound everywhere, but South Africa by no means stands alone in this respect. The West Indies are wonderful, and the keenness of the natives on cricket, as well as the novelty of the surroundings, renders a tour there most exhilarating.

In one important respect, however, all the countries visited are alike, and that is in the great kindness and hospitality shown to the tourists wherever they go, both by clubs and by individuals. It is a strenuous time indeed, but the pleasures outweigh the discomforts a hundredfold and, colouring it all, there is the proud and glorious feeling that you are honoured guests as the chosen representatives of English sportsmanship. And so the team sails for home, tired and longing for a little peace, leaving behind many friends old and new, and having enjoyed nearly everything—*except some of the cricket.*

CRICKET TOURS ABROAD

Do these Test tours do good ? Undoubtedly they have done in the past, both to visitors and visited ; educationally, socially, and politically ; individually and collectively. It would be a thousand pities if this over-anxiety to win—which mars the enjoyment of players in Test Matches and has lately caused such trouble in Australia—should ever become so accentuated as to destroy friendly relationships. They teach comparative values and create interest in the game, not only among the many thousands of actual spectators, but also among English-speaking people in all parts of the world. And there is no doubt that first-class cricket would be hard put to it financially to exist in many places without them.

Artist Unknown] [From the painting in the National Portrait Gallery

"FILLS OUR VISION AND DOES NOT FADE"
(WILLIAM GILBERT ["W. G."] GRACE)

[Frontispiece

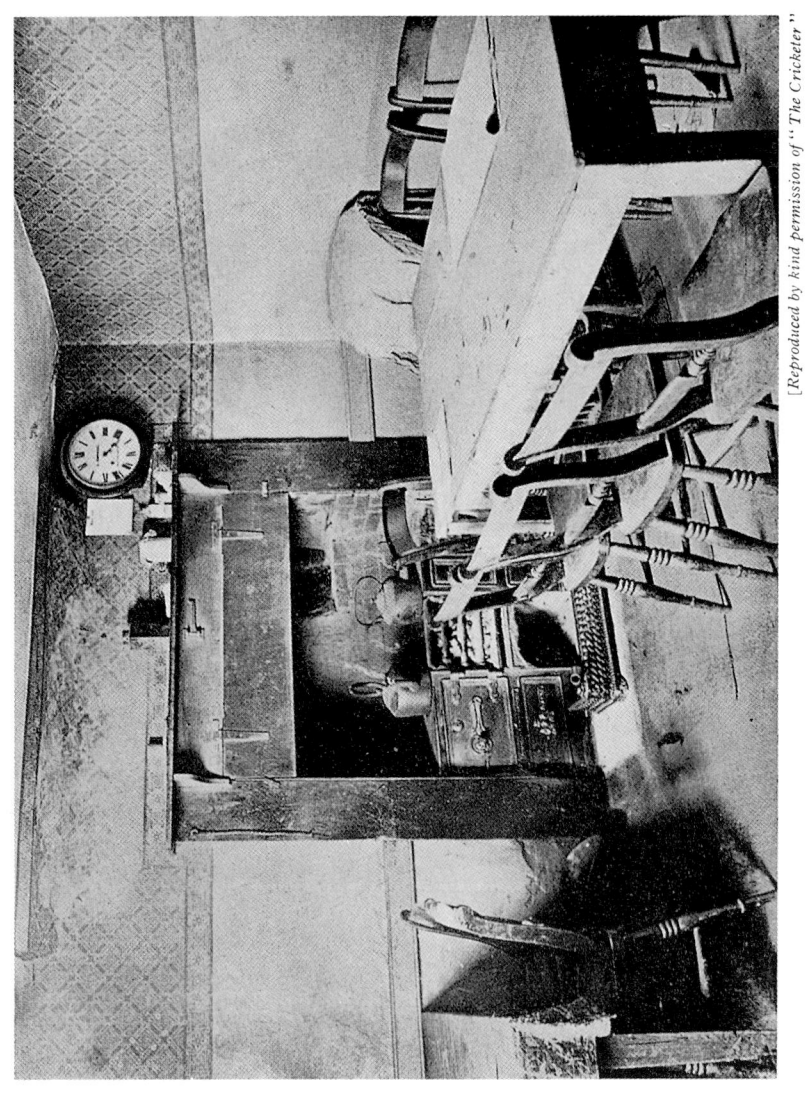

[*Reproduced by kind permission of "The Cricketer"*]

THE KITCHEN AT THE BAT AND BALL INN, HAMBLEDON

THE CRADLE OF CRICKET

A PIONEER OF MODERN BOWLING
(WILLIAM LILLYWHITE)

THE GAME GROWS UP
(DRAWING BY "RIP!")

THE BATSMAN
Fuller Pilch.

FIRST OF THE MODERN GIANTS

[*Photograph by G. W. Beldam*

THE PERFECT OFF-DRIVE
(W. G. GRACE)

[Photograph by G. W. Beldam

THE PERFECT PUSH-STROKE

(W. G. GRACE)

[Between 56-57

JUMPING OUT TO DRIVE
(VICTOR TRUMPER)

[*Photograph by G. W. Beldam*

"THE STRAIGHT DRIVE COMPLETED TO PERFECTION"
(VICTOR TRUMPER)

[*Photograph by G. W. Beldam*]

Between 64-65

HE CAPTAINED "ALL-ENGLAND"

"IN HIS FINAL STRIDE"
(S. HAIGH OF YORKSHIRE)

Photograph by G. W. Beldam

Photograph by G. W. Beldam

A WONDERFUL BALANCING FEAT . . . ON TOE AND KNEE IN THE SLIPS

("LONG JOHN" TUNNICLIFFE)

BY TOM WEBSTER
("DAILY MAIL")

"HE RECORDS ONLY THE SUNNY HOURS"
(FRANK WOOLLEY IN 1910)

Photograph by G. W. Beldam

"JUST BEFORE THE UPWARD SWING BEGINS"
(WILFRED RHODES)

[Photo by courtesy of Sport and General

"HE'S A TERROR FOR HIS SIZE"
(A. P. FREEMAN)

VIEW OF THE MARY-LE-BONE CLUB'S CRICKET GROUND

"ERE WE CAME"

(LORD'S A HUNDRED YEARS AGO)

THE CRABBLE GROUND AT DOVER
A DRAWING BY X. WILLIS ("KENTISH EXPRESS")

[Photograph by G. W. Beldam

HE SCORES TO-DAY FOR HIS COUNTY, KENT
(ALEC HEARNE BOWLING—"BOTH FEET BROUGHT TOGETHER")

[Photo by courtesy of "The Cricketer"

AT THE BEGINNING OF HIS GIANTHOOD
(JOHN BERRY HOBBS)

[Between 136-137

[*Photo Central Press, by courtesy of Victor Gollancz Ltd.*

CHAMPION OF HIS WORLD
(JACK HOBBS, THE GREAT SURREY AND ENGLAND BATSMAN)

CRICKETERS' NIGHT: BY "STRUBE" ("DAILY EXPRESS")

W. A. OLDFIELD, JACK HOBBS, TREVOR WIGNALL, C. GRIMMETT, W. O'REILLY, E. P. HENDREN, FLEETWOOD-SMITH, PARRY JONES, JOSEPH HARKER, ALAN KIPPAX, A. P. HERBERT, GORDON HARKER, HAROLD WILLIAMS, TOM CLARKE, W. A. BROWN, CLIFFORD MOLLISON. ALL THESE (PLAYERS AND OTHERS) SIGNED THE MENU-CARD

Photograph by G. W. Beldam

PREPARING FOR A DRIVE—"THE MOVEMENT OF THE FEET IS INTERESTING"
(CLEM HILL)

[*Photograph by G. W. Beldam*

"JUMPING OUT AND HITTING HIGH"
(J. H. SINCLAIR—SOUTH AFRICA)

BY TOM WEBSTER

("DAILY MAIL")

[Photograph by G. W. Beldam

THE GLANCE—" EXCLUSIVE TO 'RANJI'"
(K. S. RANJITSINHJI AT HOVE)

CRICKET AT MOULSEY HURST. THE SCENE OF SOME HAMBLEDON MATCHES.

THE GAME BEGAN TO GROW

[*Photograph by G. W. Beldam*

"NOT MERELY FOR DEFENCE"
(C. B. FRY)

"PLAYING FOR ENGLAND"
(HERBERT SUTCLIFFE)

[Photograph by G. W. Beldam

"FATHER OF MAURICE TATE"
(F. W. TATE—A JUMP BEFORE THE LAST STRIDE)

"THE MODESTY OF TRUE GREATNESS"
(VICTOR TRUMPER)

"A MATCH OF CRICKET WAS PLAID"

[Reproduced by kind permission of the M.C.C. and Sport and General

[Photograph by G. W. Beldam

"THIS IS THE HAPPY BOWLER, THIS IS HE"
(GEORGE HIRST—A SWERVER'S GRIP)

"REAL SOLID OLD-FASHIONED"
(ARTHUR SHREWSBURY)

"IN FULL SWING"
(A DRAWING BY "RIP!")

A PAGE OUT OF "WISDEN'S," 1931

SOME OLD MASTERS
(A DRAWING BY "RIP!")

[Photograph by G. W. Beldam]

HALF-WAY THROUGH THE UPSWING

(F. S. JACKSON)

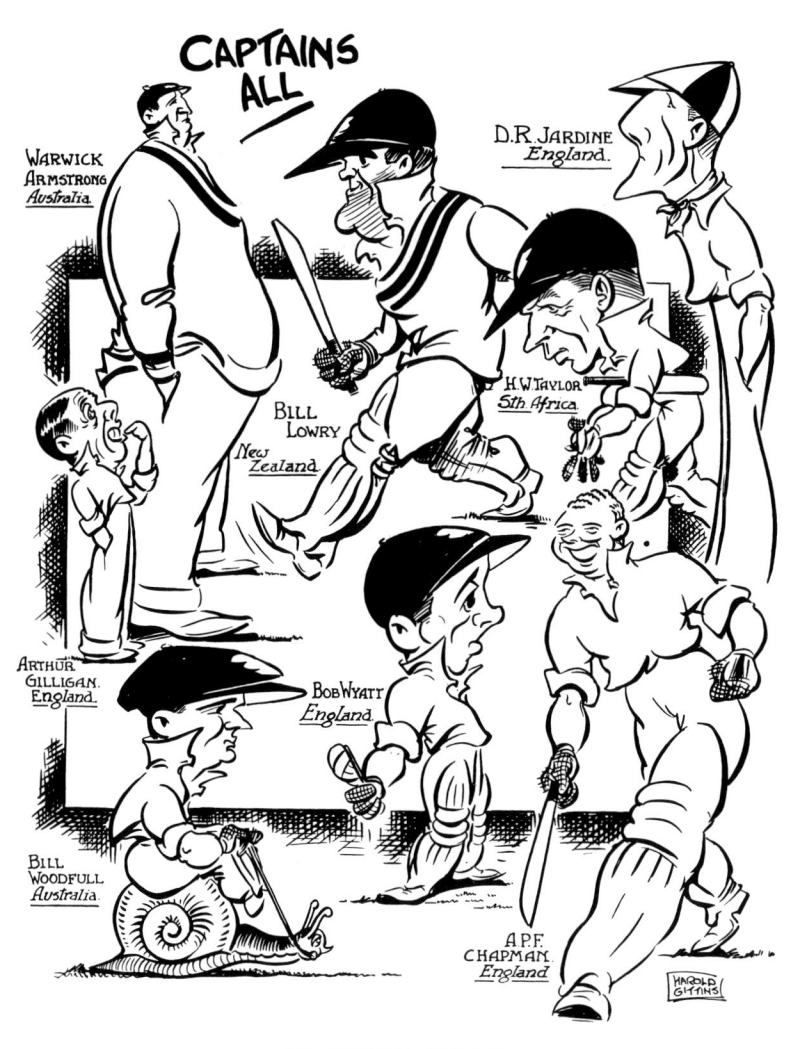

BY HAROLD GITTINS
("EVENING NEWS," LONDON)

[Photograph by G. W. Beldam
"THE RIGHT ARM AND WRIST HAVE DONE THE WORK"
(R. E. FOSTER—FINISHING A HOOK)

THE MOTE PARK, MAIDSTONE

(A DRAWING BY X. WILLIS "KENTISH EXPRESS")

CHAPTER TEN

Cricket at the Universities

BY S. J. SOUTHERTON

(Editor of *Wisden's Cricketers' Almanack* 1933-5)

CHAPTER TEN

Cricket at the Universities

BY S. J. SOUTHERTON

(Editor of *Wisden's Cricketers' Almanack* 1933–5)

CRICKET having grown for well over a hundred years to the proportions it now occupies in our national existence, one is apt to overlook in writing or talking about the game the great part in it that University players have taken.

Professional cricketers have been with us from the earliest days. I myself can remember as a child the late Fred Gale, "The Old Buffer," talking about the deeds of "Lumpy" and Billy Beldham, John Nyren, Alfred Mynn and Thomas Beagley, and, to come down to some who in comparison with these famous players can almost be described as modern men, Tarrant and Jackson, Tom Box, and John Wisden, "The Little Wonder." Whether he actually saw all these great exponents, I beg leave to doubt. That, however, is beside the question. He knew of nearly all of them and what they had accomplished just as we at the present day can talk glibly of Tom Hayward, William Gunn, Arthur Shrewsbury, Bobby Peel, Jack Hobbs, Wilfred Rhodes, and—to be right up to date—Hammond, Hendren, and Sutcliffe. But while these names are rolling off our tongues just as those of a much earlier date rolled off the tongues of our fathers and grandfathers, we are, I think, possibly a little forgetful sometimes of those wonderful University players who, not only in the matches of lesser importance at Oxford and

Cambridge, but by great deeds in *the* annual struggle at Lord's, have lifted themselves into prominence.

Not merely a chapter or two, but a whole book, could be filled by recapitulating most of the momentous happenings in the University Match alone. What bitter tragedies on the one hand, and what glorious triumphs on the other, does it recall! And yet, when all is said, the reflection is left with us that in our great national game University cricketers have played their part and the matches have furnished many noteworthy pages of its history.

This is all to the good, for it would not be well if the exponents of cricket consisted entirely of the paid player. They bat, bowl, and field well enough, and indeed in these days earn to the full the emoluments their attributes bring them. Cricket being their living, they approach it from a somewhat different standpoint than does the young undergraduate from Oxford or Cambridge, who sees in the glorious pastime a means of enjoyment, while at the same time exhibiting his prowess which, first having its birth at his prep. school, was fostered and encouraged to blossom at his public school.

There have been slow, plodding batsmen at the Universities; bowlers who, if Tritons among the minnows with their colleagues, have, against more experienced batsmen, found themselves to be just ordinary bowlers; and captains who forgot their Napoleonic ideas and schemes directly they left school to go to a Varsity. Generally speaking, however, the cricket of the "unpaid" has given that touch of lightness in bringing out the points of the game in its brightest colours which has made, and which everyone hopes will continue to make, first-class cricket the attractive spectacle we all wish it to be.

In the history of the University Match, extending back to the first meeting of the Elevens at Lord's on an early June day in 1827, when Charles Wordsworth captained

CRICKET AT THE UNIVERSITIES

Oxford, and Herbert Jenner (afterwards Jenner-Fust) led Cambridge, the astounding performances that have taken place are all too numerous to mention. But there are many interesting little points upon which it is permissible to touch in the course of this short disquisition on University Cricket.

Thus we learn that a participant in this first match was an Oxford undergraduate who, when a schoolboy at Rugby, made himself famous for evermore as the originator of Rugby football by picking up the ball and running with it. To his memory a tablet has been placed in the wall overlooking that historic playing-field at Rugby School, and on it is carved :

> THIS STONE COMMEMORATES THE EXPLOIT OF WILLIAM WEBB ELLIS, WHO, WITH A FINE DISREGARD FOR THE RULES OF FOOTBALL AS PLAYED IN HIS TIME, FIRST TOOK THE BALL IN HIS ARMS AND RAN WITH IT, THUS ORIGINATING THE DISTINCTIVE FEATURE OF THE RUGBY GAME.
> A.D. 1823.

Ellis made 12 runs for Oxford before being bowled by Jenner, but through the fact that he played in that original struggle the match must ever remain a landmark, even in the history of the winter game.

In the fifth match, we read too that Cambridge won by an innings and 125 runs, but is not some of the glamour of that victory—their first—tarnished by the very terse statement in the Oxford score : " No. 11 absent " ? What would be said in these days if all the papers came out with such an announcement as that ? But then, perhaps, we are a little more up to date, and University Elevens, like

Test Match Elevens, always have their "twelfth man" to step in in emergencies like these, as a fieldsman at any rate. History deponeth not why the eleventh man was absent.

Proceeding onwards, we come to the ninth match, played on Bullingdon Green, Oxford, in 1843, when, in windy weather and on a slippery ground, the all-round play is described as being "very fair." H. E. Moberly took seven wickets in each innings, and yet there was an aggregate of no fewer than 82 wides in the four innings against 309 runs scored from the bat. That match, like others of more recent date, when the individual doings of a player receive greater attention, might easily be called, after the man who earned most distinction—"Moberly's Match."

And now we must on with our seven-league boots, skipping over many years during which cricket in general was advancing to that stage when the first individual hundreds in University cricket began to make their appearance, and we find that in 1870 the distinction of registering the first century for his University belongs to "Bill" Yardley. Yardley, a fine hitter, in the second innings of Cambridge, scored exactly a hundred, and Cambridge won a most exciting struggle by 2 runs. This, however, was not "Yardley's Match." Oh no! It goes down to history as "Cobden's Match," for F. C. Cobden, the fast bowler of Cambridge, finished it off by doing the hat-trick in what in any case would have been the last over of the match.

Had the game taken place at the present time, columns and columns would have been written about it. At least we must assume so, provided always that those whose duty it would have been to describe the cricket could have got over their excitement by the time they reached Fleet Street. There never was such a match. First Yardley's wonderful innings at a very critical period of the game, for when he went in the Light Blues, with five men out in their second innings, were a paltry 12 runs ahead. J. W. Dale defended stubbornly, and Yardley hit the fast bowlers of Oxford in magnificent fashion; but despite all this fine work, Oxford had to get only 179 to win.

Towards this they went, thanks to A. T. Fortescue, C. J. Ottaway—a beautiful cricketer and a very handsome man—and E. F. S. Tylecote, such a long way that, although time was drawing near, they literally had the match in their hands. Then came the period when the last over was about to be sent down by F. C. Cobden, and off the first ball of it F. H. Hill, who in the end took out his bat, scored a single. The position then was that Oxford, with three wickets in hand, wanted only three runs to win. That momentous single was the most tragic ever obtained, and Hill, writing years afterwards, declared that he never regretted anything so much as running it. A. A. Bourne next made a fine catch from a hard hit by S. E. Butler, and Cobden, bowling very fast in a bad light—play by arrangement was going on until half-past seven—dismissed W. A. Stewart and T. A. Belcher with his next two deliveries, both well pitched up, did the hat-trick, pulled the match out of the fire, and enabled Cambridge to gain the most sensational victory ever recorded in the annals of Oxford and Cambridge cricket.

How often does the glory attending the achievements of one man overshadow the fine efforts of another! In all the excitement Yardley's 100 was almost forgotten, while E. E. Harrison-Ward, when Cambridge were fighting against what seemed inevitable defeat, took six wickets for 29 runs, and, with the exception of W. H. Hadow, got rid of all the best Oxford bats. Surely would not greater justice have been done if this match had gone down to history not as " Cobden's," but as that of a trilogy—" Yardley's," " Cobden's," and " Ward's " ? And now we of the present generation are left to wonder how many umbrella handles were chewed to pulp during those dramatic minutes !

The ice, so far as University Match centuries were concerned, having once been broken, hundreds followed in almost regular sequence, until the climax possibly was reached in 1931, when A. Ratcliffe played the first individual innings of over 200, but this, singularly enough, remained a record for only one day. On the next afternoon the Nawab of Pataudi scored 238 not out. Records, like eggs, are as a rule made only to be broken, and he would be a bold man who would dare to state that in these present days of wonderful batsmanship Pataudi's 238 will stand for long as the highest individual innings ever hit in the Oxford and Cambridge match.

Up to the present year of grace, there have been fifty-one individual three-figure scores, yet no batsman has succeeded in scoring two separate hundreds in the same match. Several of the century-makers subsequently went on to do great deeds in higher-class cricket such as Test Matches, and yet curiously enough there are some in the list of batting heroes of Oxford and Cambridge who, flaring up in the Varsity Match with a century, were almost unheard of afterwards.

Still, University cricket provides the historian with numberless notable features. That god of former days, W. G. Grace, did not go to either University, but had he done so, what records would he have created ? At the time when he was of the age to be an undergraduate he was not only the outstanding batsman in the world, but he was a great bowler as well, and it must always be a matter of regret that circumstances did not conspire to enable him to go to either Oxford or Cambridge. And in mentioning " W. G.", one instinctively calls to mind that his eldest son, W. G. Grace, jnr., was at Cambridge. If the truth

CRICKET AT THE UNIVERSITIES

be told, young " W. G." was not quite up to the standard of the average University cricketer. He had rather a stilted, awkward style in batting, but he took a few wickets with his somewhat angular action in bowling. Still, he was given his Blue, and thereby hangs a very sad and tragic story.

He played for Cambridge in 1895 and 1896, scoring in the first year 40 and 28 and taking one wicket. In the following season, when Oxford, left to get 330 in the last innings, hit off the runs for the loss of six wickets, I was a witness to one of the most heartbreaking scenes it has ever been my lot to encounter. " W. G." jnr. had been bowled by J. C. Hartley for nought in the first innings, and when he went in a second time, his mother and sister were sitting on the grand-stand just next to the press box. It was quite obvious to anybody watching them that they were both highly strung over the question as to how Grace would acquit himself. For the second time in the match he was bowled—on this occasion by F. H. E. Cunliffe—without scoring, and as he was making his way back to the pavilion, I glanced at Mrs. Grace and saw tears coursing down her cheeks. Her sorrow was intense, for on the ground on which her famous husband had achieved so many triumphs, the son, in the greatest match of his career, had twice failed.

That particular match was the one in which the action of Frank Mitchell, the Cambridge captain, forced the M.C.C. to reconsider the whole question of the follow-on rule. In those days the side which was 120 runs behind had, willy-nilly, to follow on. When nine Oxford wickets had fallen, Cambridge were leading by 131 runs, and, rightly or wrongly, Mitchell, as Cambridge captain, judged that it would be better for his own side to go in again than to field for the rest of the afternoon. Accordingly E. B. Shine was instructed to bowl in such a manner as would obviate the necessity of Oxford following on. He sent down three balls—two of them no-balls—which went to the boundary for four each, and those twelve runs deprived the Dark Blues of following their innings. The law is different now, for the side which leads by 150 runs in a three-days' match have the *option* of requiring the other side to follow their innings. One great change, therefore, in the laws of cricket, has been brought about by the University Match.

Reference has been made earlier in this article to the calling of a certain match " Cobden's Match," and that of 1910 is usually known as " Le Couteur's Match." Le Couteur, an Australian up at Oxford, scored 160 and took eleven Cambridge wickets for 66 runs, which can be written down as the best all-round performance in the history of the annual struggle.

While on the subject of records, it is of interest to note that there are only four instances of men twice scoring hundreds for their respective University. W. Yardley made 100 in 1870, and 130 in 1872; H. J. Enthoven scored 104 in 1924, and 129 in 1925; the Nawab of Patiala, 106 in 1929, and 238 not out in 1931; and A. Ratcliffe, 201 in 1931 and 124 in 1932. Of these, Pataudi alone was an Oxonian. To Oxford belongs the honour of hitting up the highest total—503 in 1900. They also made 453 for eight wickets in 1931, while the highest total for Cambridge is 431 in 1932.

Having made the highest total, it is only fitting that Oxford should have scored the lowest. This was 32 in 1878.

I began this chapter with some reference to the great part amateur cricketers had played in the history of cricket, and in this respect reference must be made to the performance of A. P. F. Chapman, the present Kent captain. He is the only player who has scored a century

CRICKET AT THE UNIVERSITIES

at Lord's in the University Match (102 not out for Cambridge in 1922); for Gentlemen v. Players (160 in 1922, and 108 in 1926); and for England v. Australia (121 in 1930). There, surely, is a record of which any man can be justly proud, and upon which Chapman can always look back with feelings of great personal satisfaction.

India has played no small part in the Oxford and Cambridge Match. Mention has already been made of the doings of the Nawab of Pataudi. In 1893 the greatest of all Indian cricketers, K. S. Ranjitsinhji, played for Cambridge; in 1925, 1926, and 1928, his nephew, K. S. Duleepsinhji, appeared for the Light Blues, and as recently as 1933 M. Jahangir Khan also assisted the Light Blues with distinction as a bowler.

But when one sits down and thinks of the famous players of comparatively modern years and their notable deeds, one becomes lost in admiration. Who, for instance, has made such a mark on Cambridge University cricket as S. M. J. Woods? An Australian by birth, he came to England to be educated at Brighton College; proceeded to Cambridge, and there, both at cricket and Rugby football, became the outstanding figure of his time. Truly a man. Possessed of pluck and determination that literally knew no bounds, Sam Woods, were he playing to-day as he played at the zenith of his fame, would still stand out by himself not only by reason of his prowess as batsman, bowler, and fielder at cricket, and as forward at Rugby football, but because of his lion-hearted temperament. To him a match was never lost until the last ball had been sent down or the last run made. He accomplished many great things in the University Match, although he never made a hundred in it.

Yet another Australian in B. W. Hone as recently as 1932 scored 167 against Cambridge, so that it will be seen that this particular encounter is open really to the whole world for those who are fortunate enough to go to either University and succeed as cricketers.

No account, brief though it may be, of Oxford and Cambridge cricket would be complete without reference to Sir Stanley Jackson, who, as the Hon. F. S. Jackson, played four seasons for Cambridge and was captain in 1892 and 1893. Already at Harrow he had shown that wonderfull all-round skill and ability which carried him into the University Eleven without any possible question, and later on under Lord Hawke, himself a former Cambridge captain, he accomplished wonderful deeds for Yorkshire, and then reached the height of a cricketer's fame by leading England against Australia, and moreover winning the toss on seven consecutive occasions, five of them in one season.

The great C. B. Fry played three seasons for Oxford, and was captain in 1894; Gilbert Jessop led Cambridge in 1899, having played first in 1896, and to come right down to almost the present day, D. R. Jardine, although he never captained Oxford, played for the Dark Blues for three years, but, unlike his father, M. R. Jardine, did not succeed in reaching three figures in an innings. Still, Douglas Jardine afterwards enjoyed the distinction of taking an M.C.C. team to Australia, and at his first attempt led the side to victory in four out of the five Test Matches, earning for himself the reputation of being one of the finest captains England had ever sent to that country.

So one could go on for page after page, mentioning famous University cricketers by the score or almost the hundreds, and it all goes to show what a great influence University cricket has had on the cricket of England. Not because they are amateurs; not because they are University men, but because they are of a splendid type of

CRICKET AT THE UNIVERSITIES

young manhood do we admire them all and pay tribute to their prowess.

The laws of cricket may change ; the spirit of it we hope never will, and so long as Oxford and Cambridge continue to send forth into the world these fine examples of sportsmanship, cricket will never die. They play the game for the game's sake, and in the University Match at any rate count the game itself as a far higher guerdon than the mere result. But not one of them ever goes into the field without that great desire for his side to be successful, and the success of his University probably counts with him more than individual achievement.

CHAPTER ELEVEN
Club and School Cricket
BY HUGH DE SÉLINCOURT

CHAPTER ELEVEN

Club and School Cricket

BY HUGH DE SÉLINCOURT

IT would be interesting to know exactly how many sides turn out, belonging to how many clubs, on a Saturday afternoon throughout the country. A goodish few, I'll be bound. And the amount of patient work involved in the arrangement of fixture lists, in the getting up of sides (all this work done, too, being wholly disinterested, without thought of gain, merely out of goodwill and keenness), must be enormous. Nearly always (name after name springs to my mind as I write) the man who does this work is some quiet, self-effacing, effective fellow, who does not play himself, but has the welfare of the club closely at heart. If anything goes wrong—and mistakes are bound to happen—out he comes into the limelight; no team turns up—it may not be his fault. But he is for it. He meets black looks; his keenness is considered fussiness; his goodwill ticked off as self-importance—I know many such cases. Every club should, once in a while, possess a really bad secretary, if only to be able to appreciate one whose errors are infrequent, and what those errors can mean. I never cease to be surprised at the astounding stupidity of the man who will take smooth working for granted and grumble at the slightest deviation from his own high standard of how things should be done—by somebody else. It is so damned easy to find fault. Players have groused to me about men who were heaven-sent to any club, players who ought to have known better, who ought to realise how much must go on behind the scenes before a game of cricket is possible.

BAT AND BALL

That club is lucky which has a keen secretary, and the members of that club should realise their luck, so that he gets for his pains recognition more lasting, more continual than the usual rather perfunctory tribute—" And now, Gentlemen, I have much pleasure in proposing a vote of thanks to Mr. So-and-so, our worthy Secretary . . . without whom . . ." and so on. He deserves (and should get) far more than the moment's drumming on the table with a left knife or fork, once a year at the Club's Annual Dinner.

Having tried to pay our patient secretary his due, I should like to draw his attention to a matter which again and again I have noticed sapping a good side's effectiveness, and which is apt to escape attention, because the people whom the evil primarily affects are not the people who can raise their voice in protest.

I'd often wondered vaguely, looking down, as I generally do on a Monday morning, the list of Club Matches in my paper, at the number of declarations round about 200 for three or four or five wickets. Nice little grounds, you know, with plumb wickets; and pleasant pavilions, of course, where you can sit and watch the star club batsmen playing themselves quietly in and then start enjoying a good hit. I wondered vaguely, as I say, how these excellent clubs kept their sides together, because, however pleasant it is to watch the same two or three men batting —and nobody wants anybody to get out—it is also undoubtedly pleasant occasionally to have a knock oneself. It didn't concern me very closely, and I left it at idle wonder.

But this summer it was brought home to me, and I determined, if ever I got the chance, to bring the matter up; because here is a very real grievance which those who have the interests of the good game at heart would do well very seriously to consider.

CLUB AND SCHOOL CRICKET

I was playing for a very nice side in August on the south coast, who entertain a number of touring teams. On one occasion, there opened the innings for us a young fellow, home on holiday from London, where he worked. Lord! how that fellow enjoyed a game of cricket! You could tell it from the moment he began to put his pads on, watch it as he walked out to the wicket. For a quarter to half an hour he played himself very carefully in, remaining in the early teens; then he opened out and steadily, fiercely attacked the bowling—into the sixties well within the hour: there was nothing wild about his play, no aimless slogging, but concentrated attack, hard driving, swift hooking, and any ball short of a length smitten with quick strong wrists on either side of a backward point. He came back to the pavilion, beaming, caught off a skier.

" Gosh! I enjoyed that knock; it's the first I've had this year."

" Why? Can't you get a game in London? "

" Oh! yes. I play for [he mentioned a well-known club], but I never get a knock. Well, twice, as a matter of fact; I'm six or seven, and each time the skipper said: 'Just hit at everything, see; it's runs we want before I declare!' It doesn't give you a chance. Still, I keep wicket, so I get some fun there."

Now that shows a stupid state of affairs which does damage to the club and could with a little forethought be quite easily avoided. The side as a whole suffers from the excellence of the few. The keen youngster is apt to drift away to some club less excellent but more amusing, where he gets a chance which could easily have been given him in the better club. The main body of the team begins to sag. The interest goes from the games. The wrong men are attracted.

I had a striking example last summer of the difference a damped side, by which I mean eight men permitted to turn out with three superlative players, and a keen side, all together, makes for the whole enjoyment of the game.

The damped side was skippered by a man who had played for his county—an admirable all-rounder. It should have been a thrilling match (the winning hit was made in the last over) ; it was merely a maddening one. The atmosphere was foggy and thick, though the sun rode high. There was something impalpably wrong somewhere with the whole thing ; a sort of discomfort was noticeable from the very start, and, as the day wore on, grew to open resentment when, with the clock to beat, the general pottering and delay in changing the bowling and setting the field became too manifest. The colloquies on tactics between the great man and his stumper would have been less out of place in a timeless test ; and there was no barracker stout-lunged and rude enough to whip them out of their deliberations.

It is a queer thing how the enjoyment of a game suffers from the lack of corporate feeling on one side. Its bad influence is infectious. A host of little things, none by itself of any importance, none by itself mischievous (rather late start, too long wait between batsmen, careless return of the ball, a pervasive growing slackness in the field, and so on), in their accumulation serve to ruin an afternoon. And the mischief is to be traced as often as not to two or three outstanding players in a club who, without themselves realising it, bulk far too largely for the side's corporate health. Not always does the outstanding player depress the side's personality : I have known instances (delightful to remember) in which the exact contrary happened and the whole side seemed galvanised and glowing with the great one's presence in their midst. But it is a very great danger from which a lot of high-class clubs suffer and which those in authority would do well to face and overcome.

Pleasanter far to record another game which draws

attention to the absurdity of those croakers who assure us that interest in cricket is on the wane. Nothing of the sort. Interest is spreading ; and interest of the right kind, as evidenced in a side known as The Triflers, who tour on the south coast and have the good fortune to possess a private home ground. On various occasions I have had the luck to play against that side—which varies in strength, rightly enough, with the calibre of the team to which it is opposed ; but on every occasion one point was manifest from the moment they stepped on to the field, whatever the strength of the side—and this one point was keenness. In the field, they were on their toes, backing up, nipping in to the ball, returning it neatly and cleanly and at once ; all the little so important finer points were known and practised, not by one or two, but by the whole side—and occasionally there were brilliant bits of fielding, as must happen when the ball-to-ball routine is neatly and swiftly performed. The running between the wickets, when the side was batting, was always alive and right—in calling, in backing up, in prompt running. It was good to watch, refreshing, and pleasant. There is a sort of spurious affability which can make a game sag. It is the bane really of club cricket. Slack running, slack fielding. After all, what's it matter ?—and the whole game is let down and becomes the most penitential waste of time. Given the right sort of keenness—which this side showed to such perfection that I longed for them to go about playing all over the countryside giving a perfect exhibition of how the game should be played—there is a spirit generated so strong and fine, that it puts meaning even into that much-abused phrase—" It's not cricket."

All clubs without exception should see that the routine of the game is neatly and swiftly carried out ; little matters such as the prompt return of the ball to the bowler, smart calling between wickets, the outgoing batsman crossing the incoming batsman, and many more should be insisted upon; on attention to them depends the enjoyment of the game.

The ball is hit to cover—a great man who has played for his county. There is no chance of a run; cover strolls in, picks up the ball, gives himself a catch or two, jerks a trick catch to the bowler, who misses it, and the ball knocks the bails off—the umpire laughs and chats with the bowler while he puts them on again. The great man makes some jesting apology, gets back to his place, the game goes on.

I've seen it happen. All very friendly and genial, and so nice of the great man not to put on side, don't you know, but to be jolly with the chaps. . . . Yes (and I say it in all seriousness); he lets the side down by this slack foolishness worse than the worst rabbit, who is doing his lapinian best. An abomination far too often seen on the field. For in my opinion no game can be so excellent as cricket when it is properly played; and no game, when it is slackly played, can be quite so abominably feeble.

Naughty little boys jeered a player who was too languid in his pursuit of a ball; to their intense delight, he walked after the next one that came his way.

And that takes me straight, bang, from club cricket, which is apt to err on the genial lazy side, to school cricket, which is apt to err, especially among the very young, on the strenuous serious side. Our glorious fellow who registered his resentment of the small boy's hoots by walking after the ball was really doing nothing of the kind: he was asserting himself at long last against past enforced discipline which had been too severe for his self-respect. He felt quite a man at last instead of merely a bullied automaton as he strolled after the ball on our ground to the accompaniment of shrill ribaldry. He was quite unaware, poor chap, of being the most conspicuous ass. You do not see many quite such glaring examples of the mischief of over-strictness; but the number of well-drilled automata, good little machines without punch or personality, in the best class of cricket is painful and astonishing to contemplate. All the fun and fury have been drilled out of them, both as batsmen and bowlers. Their play lacks devilment, lacks attack; they are content to avoid mistakes, to stop in, or to keep down the runs—all to the book, see page so-and-so written all over them. Or else, if they should be called upon to hit, out they go, reckless and stiff and silly, a sight as deplorable as their usual defensive patting, shot after shot after shot which could never under any circumstances score a run, when the same shot played with looseness and power and equal safety would be good for a four every time. Stylish ball-stopping is mistaken for batting. The field is set for this stylish imbecility where to hit the ball hard is regarded as an outrage, as an obscenity. We were playing the Club and Ground. A pleasant medium-paced bowler had his field placed for our awe of the occasion : no one in the deep : men crowding up, silly on silly, for correctness that was not quite correct enough. I went trembling in to bat—against such cricketers ! Two were playing for the county next day, and old George Cox was there—Oh, well, dash it ! one looked, quaking, round; the littlest hit'll be safe as a well-built house. So out I shuffled, awed and afraid, took a half-hearted smack, scooped an awful shot, evoking a general pitying smile, but perfectly safe for two by mid-wicket. So a man was at once put there. I was less timorous for the next, but pulled it—for four over mid-on's head. So a man went there too, wider happily than the shot I like—and, not greatly minding the superior smile, I got hold of the next, and it went hard and straight, where I like 'em to go, between mid-off and the bowler. I hold, well remembering the superior smile, that those shots, the most wavering attack, were *safer* than the stylish protective pat. To my mind it was impudence of that bowler not to have a couple of men in the deep, far greater impudence than mine in having a go with the field set as it was, and runs very badly wanted.

Let me emphasise the point with rudeness, and declare that a Hammond suffering from the Grimmetts in a Test is indistinguishable from hundreds of other little first-class protective Pats, except that his ailment flatters the bowler into superhuman power and cunning of attack.

Our young players rarely get free of coaching and the coach to assert their own individual genius. The evil goes right back to the earliest days. I have insisted before, and I shall continue to insist whenever I can get (or make) the chance, that cricket is not a game that commends itself to the very young. They find it dull ; and for them it is dull. They want to be all out in a game, all the time ; and they cannot be all out any of the time. It is all too difficult. They want fun and excitement, which are the essence of a game, and they are right to want fun and excitement. The livelier the little boy, the more bored he gets with the whole dreary business. He must put aside his devilment and mischief and be a good little obedient chap and learn how to pick up the ball, how to throw it in, how to hold his bat, how to stand, where to stand, and so on and so on—worse than the Latin Grammar or Fractions, which at any rate are not supposed to be amusing. It is not surprising that the liveliest young 'uns develop a sort of horror for the game ; rather is it surprising that any young 'uns survive this doleful initiation, and show later on any spirit at all.

And the answer to the problem is simple ; it stares us in the eye, though it sounds almost blasphemy to mention it. Face after earnest face of perfect young men, admirable Games Masters at admirable Preps, loom shocked before my mind as I write the words, but undaunted I write them ; and they are : *Little Boys should be taught cricket by means of Tip and Run.* They want FUN; at Tip and Run, they get it. They want to be all out, all the time. They are all out at Tip and Run and all the time. Eight a side they should play, with a pitch of twelve to fifteen yards. Everyone should bowl in rotation, unless anyone prefers not to. The most workable rules would soon be evolved, after a very few games. Sneaks should be rigorously barred by making any ball bowled that bounced more than once a No BALL.

The point is that out of the jolly breathless scramble would emerge small people keen and able to appreciate the finer points of the better game, having been properly inoculated with the incomparable fun to be had from playing with a moving ball.

There would be something for the coach, too, to catch hold of—in some youth fiercely anxious to learn from his teaching how to get the ball harder and oftener and safelier whizzing to the boundary. After all, generations of experts have evolved the delicate beauty of the cricket bat primarily for that good end, to hit a cricket ball; and not, as you might be led to suppose after watching our obedient little overdrilled players, as the best instrument with which to stop a moving ball dead when padded legs are unavailable.

I have watched a first-class opening batsman for the first hour of the game, and more than three-quarters of the balls bowled he allowed to strike against a dead bat. They put on a slow bowler to tempt him to hit; they did really. It was like sending out a cordon of police to keep the Monument from dancing—a waste of time. He couldn't. There was no fun in him; only an infinite patience.

Let young 'uns be initiated into the mysteries of the great game by the breathless excitement of that maddest of mad scrambles, Tip and Run; and that earnest gloom which is apt to descend upon the cricket field like some awful fog will be for ever dissipated.

On one occasion this gloom was so thick that a player was constrained to take illegitimate means to disperse it. He was a bowler, and he took the field after tea with a doughnut concealed in his large left hand. It was an austere match on a home ground where the authorities hoped to entice the County for a week. The cricket was of a seriousness! That bowler delivered the first ball, a slow high full toss, wide of the wicket on the leg side—the batsman smote it full and hard—smash! It was the doughnut.

An asinine act! but wickedly ridiculous. It was impossible not to laugh and laugh until one ached with laughter. But the game was ruined. The skipper batting was furious—and rightly. It was too unsettling. Three quick wickets fell.

The incident shows to what depths we have sunk when any player has recourse to such idiocy to extract a little fun out of such a game as cricket. Spurious earnestness is as much against the spirit of the game as this prize idiocy.

It paralyses bowling, though not quite so obviously. Bowling lacks character and initiative; it lacks attack and intention. The bowler is far too apt to be content with keeping down the runs. The standard of bowling is really ludicrously low, especially among amateurs who should excel. They have opportunities at school of which no use is made, opportunities of space, mainly.

There is an immense amount of work a bowler can do (and do better) without the paraphernalia of net and batsman and so on, for which he must wait for the summer term and the cricket season. All he wants is a pitch, a couple of stumps, and a friend, in order that he can learn to find his length, to spin the ball, and to vary his pace slightly without changing his action. He cannot become proficient in these delicate matters without constant practice: ground work which must be slowly built up. But what happens? He starts off bowling at his first net, in no condition, with the result that for days he is too stiff for any control over the ball: and the all-too-short season slips by before he has found his own self-confidence to avoid bowling vilely; he never gets the groundwork accomplishment on which confidence can grow, so that he is able to bowl with intention and attack. The essentials of good bowling, length and slight continual variation of pace and spin, can be acquired by constant practice and by constant practice alone. The bowler who has a soft, untrained stomach is an ass pure and simple, like a motorist who starts off with flat tyres.

He can do the groundwork of his practice all through the spring term, as I have pointed out in detail in *Over*, and he can start the all-too-brief season in bodily trim, having found his length—like a pianist or a fiddler or any other artist, properly prepared for performance. For this scale-work of bowling, a batsman is definitely not wanted—he is in the way: the bowler needs to see exactly where the ball pitches and how it leaves the pitch.

A keen kid or two of intelligence will hop on to the sense of this, and realising what an immense amount he can do on his own initiative, will raise the whole standard of bowling. He will show what a body well trained with intelligence can do, and how the art of bowling is still in its infancy.

* * * * *

My first intention was to give definite information about clubs. But their name is legion. Occupation (most large firms run a cricket club)—banks, stores, and so on. Locality—every town, every district of every town, has its club; there are old boys' clubs from every school and college throughout the kingdom; and clubs like I Zingari, Authentics, or Band of Brothers, to wear whose colours is a distinction. The records of each club would make an interesting volume by itself to brood over of a winter evening ; what might be gathered of such vast material into one short chapter would be tiresome in its sketchiness and uninteresting. The same holds good of the schools throughout the kingdom, at which cricket is played.

So it occurred to me to make use of the space at my disposal by writing not so much about particular clubs or schools as about what would be likely to be of interest and possibly of value to any player, to whatever club or school he happened to belong.

CHAPTER TWELVE

"*The Most Thrilling Finish I have ever Seen*"

BY NINE FAMOUS CRICKET WRITERS

1. ENTER HOBBS—AND J. N. CRAWFORD
    BY H. J. HENLEY ("Watchman" of the *Observer*)
2. LAST MAN IN, TWELVE MINUTES TO GO . . .
    BY WILLIAM POLLOCK ("Googly" of the *Daily Express*)
3. TWO ENGLAND VICTORIES
    BY IVAN SHARPE (*Sunday Chronicle*)
4. BY ONE WICKET
    BY FRANK THOROGOOD (*News-Chronicle*)
5. IT HAPPENED AT SCHOOL
    BY R. C. ROBERTSON-GLASGOW (*Morning Post*)
6. AND THE CAPTAIN TURNED A SOMERSAULT ON THE PITCH!
    BY J. A. H. CATTON ("Tityrus" of the *Athletic News*)
7. WHEN ENGLAND WANTED 8 RUNS
    BY NEVILLE CARDUS ("Cricketer" of the *Manchester Guardian*)
8. BEATING THE CLOCK
    BY R. B. ("BEAU") VINCENT (*The Times*)
9. NOT A SOUL STIRRED . . .
    BY H. A. H. CARSON (*Evening News,* London)

CHAPTER TWELVE

" The Most Thrilling Finish I have ever Seen "

BY SEVEN FAMOUS CRICKET WRITERS

ENTER HOBBS—AND J. N. CRAWFORD

BY H. J. HENLEY

THE most thrilling finish? Ah! there are so many kinds of thrill—the swinging century that beats the clock, the critical hour the " rabbit " stays and plays out time, the quick wickets that win the game by a run. Which will you have? Reasoned selection is impossible. Let me draw haphazard from the lucky bag of memory and see what comes out. Good! It's a fine prize. This is it :

The Oval late in the afternoon of a bleak, grey day, fifteen years ago, with rain coming up and the light bad. Surrey set 95 to beat Kent, and under three-quarters of an hour remaining. " They can't do it. They won't try. Another rotten draw. What's the good of waiting ? " So were the dirges sounded. Enter Hobbs, slim and trim, and J. N. Crawford, beautifully built ; strong and square, with eyes that see the ball perfectly through big spectacles. Crawford starts at once. Bang! The ball against the rails again. " They're going for 'em after all ! "

But Hobbs is quiet. " Why doesn't he get a move on ? " Now, he is off. . . . " He's getting 'em quicker than Crawford. 'Nother four. Hurray ! " . . . " Will they do it ? " Yes. No. Yes. No. Yes. " They are doing it. They're doing it easy. They've done it—with a good ten minutes to spare."

Then came the cheers, and the rain. Think of it—95

runs in half an hour in a wretched light against varied bowling and the best fielding side in the country. Think of it, and let the trumpets sound !

LAST MAN IN, TWELVE MINUTES TO GO . . .

BY WILLIAM POLLOCK

Trent Bridge cricket ground on the evening of June 12th, 1934. Thirty thousand people, tense in the heat ; sixty thousand eyes riveted on England's last two batsmen.

Twelve minutes to go. Can Yorkshire's Verity and Derbyshire's Mitchell keep up their wickets and so save the first Test Match ?

" Over " . . . and the Australians running to their places to save time.

Grimmett—one, two, *hop*—bowls to Verity. The batsman makes a stroke and has a momentary mind to snatch a run.

" Go back—*you fool* ! " shouts someone, overwrought, in the crowd. It is almost a sob. Quite unconscious of what I am doing, I get hold of my railway ticket in my pocket and bend it and twist it in a moist hand.

Eleven minutes to go. O'Reilly bowling now to Mitchell, running at full gallop. The crowd is very quiet, almost holding its breath.

Suddenly a tremendous shout from the bowler.

" How's that ? " He leaps into the air, his arm thrown up in excited appeal.

The umpire's finger goes up. " Out." O'Reilly, not knowing what he is doing, grabs the umpire's hand and shakes it.

Beside themselves with delight and excitement the Australians seize the stumps as souvenirs and race to the pavilion.

* * * * *

"THE MOST THRILLING FINISH"

Half an hour later, rushing to catch my train to London, the collector shakes his head at my ticket.

"You can't travel on this, sir. Look at it—you've rubbed all the printing off it."

TWO ENGLAND VICTORIES

BY IVAN SHARPE

I

Kennington Oval, 1926.—The match to decide the fate of the Ashes. England 280, Australia 302. Then rain overnight.

Now Hobbs and Sutcliffe on the treacherous Oval wicket playing each ball as though life itself depended on the outcome. Slowly, oh, so slowly, they see things through—then they reach a hundred apiece, and Australia are left to get 415 to win.

Wilfred Rhodes, whose age was nearly 49, goes out to bowl with young Harold Larwood, and they complete the kill. The Ashes are England's. . . .

II

Trent Bridge, 1930.—England *v.* Australia again. The last day's play in the first Test Match.

Another see-saw. England may win, Australia may win or save the game.

Bradman is out! England *can* win if only this defiant Fairfax, who is batting so cautiously, can be removed.

Maurice Tate (he bowled fifty overs in the first innings!) sends one down on the leg side. Fairfax sweeps it to square-leg—about the only time this six-footer Cornstalk opened his shoulders all through the Tests! . . .

Only one man afield could have reached the catch—R. W. V. Robins.

BAT AND BALL

He flies along the boundary, leaps in the air, and holds it, chest high. . . . The match is won and lost. First blood to England!

BY ONE WICKET

BY FRANK THOROGOOD

The scene is Kennington Oval in the August of 1902. England need 15 to beat Australia, with one wicket to fall, and Rhodes joins Hirst. The clock ticks on, and at ten minutes past four only 8 are needed.

A single to Hirst, another single to Rhodes, and yet another to old George, whose brain is packed in ice. Then Hirst gets 2 more as the result of a wild overthrow. Facing the same bowler—Noble—he gets another single and we want 2 to win!

Strong men hide their faces and the aged gasometer sweats blood. Noble rolls the ball in a little heap of sawdust and bends down as if he were making private terms with the international leather. "Monty" sends up the sixth delivery from the Vauxhall end wide of the off stump. But the wily Rhodes declines to nibble.

Last scene of all: Hugh Trumble bowling the final over, amid the silence of the tomb. Hirst with a single ties the match and then Rhodes brings the long tension to an end with another single, more priceless than rubies and sweeter than the honeycomb. A gentle rain descends and the crowd rolls like a mighty wave to the wicket-gate of the pavilion. England has triumphed by one wicket.

A few hours later I seek relief for shattered nerves in a London theatre, and my distinguished companion, still in a high fever, is James Catton. Does he remember it? Yes, I think so.

"THE MOST THRILLING FINISH"

IT HAPPENED AT SCHOOL

BY R. C. ROBERTSON-GLASGOW

It was over twenty years ago, in a match between two schools in Surrey; first schools, where you learn to wash and speak the truth and to worship great athletes. It was on their ground, where they had always won; a lovely pitch, a long and nervous walk to it, pine-trees, and a hot, blue sky.

We won the toss and put them in, after a journey by train and horse-brake that was in itself a match of a kind. Let us be honest. Their side was good; not, perhaps, for them, with their long tradition of sons of notable cricketers, but far better than ours. Yet at last fate flung at their batsmen what newspapers like to call "unaccountable failure," what *we* know to be cricket's way of correcting pride.

On this perfect surface, "with all appliances and means" to score, they collapsed, at first, at middle, and at last—all out 59. The chance had come, so easy a chance that it was almost frightening—remember how delicately the mind of a boy is swayed in confidence or despair.

After an early tea our opening pair began. Out there they threw off nervousness, and with calm orthodoxy took the score to exactly 30. Then a wicket fell. Two more fell for nothing. At 43, five had gone. Seventeen to win. A contemptible amount. But, with half the side gone, a mountain.

Number One batsman was still there. He was joined by Number Seven, a good boxer, but a poor and swishing bat. The boxer was persuaded to defend. By French cricket and fortune he stayed. Those seventeen were scored so easily that past fears seemed ludicrous.

We won by five wickets; yet it was the most exciting

finish that I have ever known. And I was in at it, too, begging your pardon.

THE CAPTAIN TURNED A SOMERSAULT ON THE PITCH!
BY J. A. H. CATTON

During July 1885, playing at Trent Bridge against Notts, at the height of their fame Yorkshire scored 424, which in those days was a very high total. Notts were defeated by an innings and 28 runs. Only three times previously had Yorkshire won this fixture. And never again were Notts beaten during that season.

When the last wicket fell the Yorkshire eleven threw their caps in the air, Joe Hunter jumped over the stumps, and Tom Emmett, the captain, turned a somersault on the pitch! How dared they be so exultant and so inconsiderate of the fallen foe? In our time players would never dream of such a rude demonstration. Turn a somersault on the wicket? Preposterous: the player might disturb the crease of his trousers.

Years ago when a wicket fell cricketers used to throw long and high catches to one another. These expressed rising spirit; and hope and enthusiasm. To-day if a bowler took three wickets with three balls three times in one innings, or if a batsman made a drive to the top of the gasometer at Kennington, the players would try to look as if such feats were daily events. And a Tom Emmett would now be called a clown cricketer. What is a game? Give us joy and fun.

WHEN ENGLAND WANTED 8 RUNS
BY NEVILLE CARDUS

The most thrilling finish I have ever seen was the famous Australian victory over England at Old Trafford in July 1902—by 3 runs.

"THE MOST THRILLING FINISH"

Strong men could not look the match in the face that day. I was only a schoolboy, and I can still feel on my forehead the sense of the hard iron rail that ran round the ground and against which I pressed my forehead as I prayed for poor Fred Tate—" O Lord, make him hit two fours and win England the rubber."

Maurice Tate's father came out to bat when England wanted eight runs; he was the last man; at the other end of the wicket was Wilfred Rhodes. The Australians saw to it that Rhodes did not have the opportunity of scoring again; Tate was their obvious prey.

The climax made the afternoon a scourge for all of us. England had gone in before lunch assured of the rubber —a mere 124 to win, and such batsmen to get them, despite a sticky wicket: Maclaren, Palairet, Johnny Tyldesley, " Ranji," F. S. Jackson, Abel, Braund, Lilley, Lockwood, and Rhodes. The third wicket fell at 96; Maclaren threw his innings away trying to force the runs because of the threatening weather. He thought the rain might deprive England of their spoils. None of us dreamed of defeat. The cat was out of the bag when we saw the helplessness of " Ranji " against Trumble, who bowled glorious off-breaks from round the wicket. Then Clement Hill ran twenty yards and caught Lilley from a noble drive; Hill gripped the ball and turned two somersaults. Now entered the arena the luckless Tate; he saw Rhodes deal coolly with three balls. At that moment of torment a cloudburst stopped play for forty minutes; and all the time the sun was shining not far away. Tate sat in the dressing-room in his pads and died many deaths.

At five minutes to five the Australians came into the field, grim and silent. Tate got down on his bat. But the Australian captain, Joe Darling, delayed the action while he set his field so scrupulously that Tate might have possessed a hundred scoring strokes. Darling moved his men with waves of the hand calculated to an inch. Bluff—intended to get on Tate's nerves. At last, Saunders bowled. Tate saw the ball pitch and stabbed his bat. Four off the edge. Morally out, but a boundary. Another stroke like that, no better and no worse, and Tate would go down to history as a hero. The next ball pitched a perfect length; it broke from the leg stump; it also shot—and sent the off stump flying. The crowd shuddered; the Australians leaped into the air. We all went sadly home, shaken to our foundations.

But that evening in the setting sun, a number of small boys played the finish all over again in miniature; and we saw to it this time that Rhodes got the bowling and won the rubber for England.

BEATING THE CLOCK
BY R. B. ("BEAU") VINCENT

The most exciting finish which I have seen for many years was not provided by the players, but by my own stupid self.

I may in fact be said to have felt rather than observed the excitement. It arose in this way, and only shows what anxious moments we reporters do have to survive. The occasion was a match between Sussex and Yorkshire on that, to me, most intimate and homely of grounds, Brighton —or as the meticulous will have it, Hove. The actual facts do not affect the case. Sufficient is it to say that one side had to score in a limited period at the end of the last day a certain amount of runs at a rate of one a minute to win. The Press-box was all agog; we had placed our watches each in front of our eyes on the desk until the small hut sounded for all the world like a clock-maker's shop. After an hour of great thrill I announced to my colleagues that the batting side was falling far short of its task. I was

"THE MOST THRILLING FINISH"

contradicted; and there followed considerable mathematical argument, until one bright gentleman discovered that I had lapsed into the metric system by allowing 100 minutes to the hour. It was a great blow to my vanity, but a source of amusement to my friends.

NOT A SOUL STIRRED . . .

BY H. A. H. CARSON

"For now sits Expectation in the air." *Henry V*

When asked, What interest lies in a cricket match? I answer None. As a cricketer I know that no one who could ask such a question could understand the answer, and as a spectator I realise that a cricket match only has its moments of interest.

We go to matches and nothing happens, and we go again because we know we are on the edge of circumstance, the verge of the unexpected, and would not miss what might be a life-long memory.

I missed that famous innings of Gilbert Jessop that won a Test Match at The Oval and I had and have no excuse.

There are bits of matches seen in recent years that will never be forgotten by me. First a drawn game between Oxford and Cambridge in 1928. Cambridge looked to be winning, when at half-past six the last man, E. T. Benson, joined C. K. Hill-Wood and these two played out time until seven o'clock and saved the match. There were ten thousand people there that afternoon, and for the last half-hour not a soul stirred and scarcely a word was spoken.

In 1934 in the Test Match played at Manchester, O'Reilly, the famous Australian bowler, had C. F. Walters caught off the first ball of an over, bowled R. E. S. Wyatt with the next ball, and after having the third ball snicked to leg for four, he bowled Hammond with the fourth.

BAT AND BALL

England instead of 68 runs on the board for no wicket had three wickets down for 72.

That over was worth seeing, the match was not!

The last example is also from 1934 cricket. D. G. Bradman played a miraculous hundred against Middlesex and I overheard a spectator say : " Now I have seen that I need never watch cricket again. I can go and fish with a quiet conscience."

CHAPTER THIRTEEN
Some Personalities of the Game

BY P. F. WARNER

CHAPTER THIRTEEN

Some Personalities of the Game

BY P. F. WARNER

I

W. G. GRACE

VERY few of the modern generation of cricketers have seen W. G. Grace play, and some of them are apt to question his supremacy, and to ask, rather disparagingly, if he really was as good as the best of the modern batsmen. One famous cricketer is said to have gone even so far as to suggest that if he played to-day he would not be conspicuously successful !

I first saw W. G. play in 1887, and I first played with him in 1894, when he was forty-six years of age, and when he was no longer light in figure. Later, I had the distinction of going in first with him on more than one occasion, and all I can say is that, judging him on his form when he was fifty years of age, and older, he must have been a most extraordinary batsman when he was a young man. One is apt to forget that in his youth he was, apart from his cricket, an extremely fine athlete, slim, and active enough, according to *Cricket Scores and Biographies*, to win some sixty or seventy cups.

I will quote only one instance to prove how active he must have been in his youth. On July 31st, 1866, he won the 440 yards Hurdle Race over twenty flights of hurdles—in 1 minute 10 seconds—at the Crystal Palace, and on the same day, playing for Surrey *v.* England, at the Oval, he scored 224 not out.

He could also throw a cricket ball 122 yards. This sort of thing implies extreme activity and suppleness, and it is a great pity that there is no generally known portrait or photograph of W. G. Grace as he was in the 'seventies or early 'eighties, when he was in his absolute prime. Too apt are the moderns to judge him by the photographs of him when he weighed eighteen stone: " Can a man of such huge bulk," they argue, " have been a great cricketer?" Well, he was certainly a great batsman when I saw him, when he " bulked large," and all his contemporaries are agreed that, in his youth, he was second to no one. Individuals do not have the title of " Champion " bestowed on them, in any generation, without good reason.

W. G. began his first-class cricket career when he was fifteen, and a few days before his sixteenth birthday he scored 170 and 56 not out for the South Wales Club against the Gentlemen of Sussex, at Hove. He first played for the Gentlemen against the Players when he was sixteen and he continued doing so until he was well over fifty. In his Jubilee year, 1898, he scored 126 out of 203 against C. J. Kortright, probably the fastest bowler that ever lived.

To the end of his days, Grace was supreme in playing fast bowling; he simply revelled in it, and though with increasing weight he never was so certain against slow bowling, I cannot imagine that in his youth he could not play any bowling whatever its style and pace. I once asked him which, if any, was the type of bowling he liked least, and his reply was, " I didn't care what they bowled if I was in form, but the faster they bowled, the better I liked them."

In estimating his wonderful performance—he scored 54,896 in first-class cricket—it must be remembered that the majority of the wickets in his day were nothing like so good as they are now.

He was not a stylist like Woolley or Hobbs or Lionel

SOME PERSONALITIES OF THE GAME

Palairet, but, as Ranji wrote in *The Jubilee Book of Cricket*, he revolutionised cricket. He united in his mighty self all the good points of all the good players, and made utility the criterion of style. His batting represented force, rather than a classical method, but he had every stroke. In fact, as J. C. Shaw, the famous Nottinghamshire bowler of the 'seventies, said, " I puts 'em where I likes, and he puts 'em where he likes." Even in his old age he was a magnificent late cutter, and his on driving and pulling were outstanding.

Cricketers may come, and cricketers may go, but it may be said, without any fear of contradiction whatsoever, that there never has been, and never will be, a greater personality. Imagine a man, 6 ft. 1 in. or 6 ft. 2 in., weighing, as I knew him, seventeen or eighteen stone, with a great black beard, crowned by an M.C.C. cap, with huge hands, and huge feet—feet so enormous that when he was in Australia one of the newspapers remarked that he " would be worth £3 a week and his ' tucker ' merely to walk about the district and crush the vermin" that were at that time destroying the crops in Australia. No one having once seen W. G. Grace could ever forget him ; he was as well known by sight as any man in England. You simply could not mistake him, and he dominated the cricket world for over forty years. He was the Champion, and the Champion he will remain until the end of time.

Those who are inclined to doubt his magnificence should look up his complete record and not forget that in 1895, when he was just under forty-seven years of age, he secured over a thousand runs in May. He was the glory and the pride of English cricket and cricketers.

W. G. enjoyed so many triumphs that it is impossible to pick out his greatest, but I imagine that the happiest day of his cricketing life was July 18th, 1898, his fiftieth birthday. The M.C.C. Committee had arranged the

Gentlemen *v.* Players Match at Lord's to begin on that date, and when he led the Gentlemen into the field, every one in the pavilion, and indeed, on the ground, stood up and cheered him to the echo. W. G. is said to have smiled throughout the three days, and the cricket was worthy of the occasion, the " Old Man," as he was affectionately called, himself playing no mean part in it, an innings of 43 on a difficult wicket, against Lockwood, J. T. Hearne, and Haigh, being remembered to this day by those who saw it.

Nor must it be forgotten that W. G. was also a bowler, good enough to obtain 2,864 wickets during his career, and, as late as 1902, to take five wickets for 29 runs, at Lord's, for the M.C.C. against an Australian XI, which included Trumper, Duff, Hill, Darling, Noble, S. E. Gregory, and Armstrong. In his youth, W. G. could field anywhere and catch anything, and in his old age he stood at point, or backward point, and few catches indeed escaped those enormous paws of his.

He was a great and cheery personality, with tremendous vitality and enthusiasm. He was apt, perhaps, to bully the umpires, but it must be remembered that he was an anomaly in the game of cricket. He made modern cricket; he was cricket; he popularised it. Before his day the number of spectators at matches was comparatively small. He it was who drew people to our cricket grounds ; he it was who sent the name of cricket through the length and breadth of the land, and, indeed, into every corner of the world.

He epitomised a nation's devotion to a game. Even a bishop wrote of him, " Had Grace been born in ancient Greece, the Iliad would have been a different book; had he lived in the Middle Ages, he would have been a Crusader, and would now have been lying with his legs crossed in some ancient Abbey, having founded a great family. As he was born when the world was older, he was the best known of all Englishmen, and the king of that English game least spoilt by any form of vice."

II

VICTOR TRUMPER

Victor Trumper died on June 28th, 1915, and even in the midst of the greatest war the world has ever known the newspapers found space to record at great length the genius of this marvellous batsman. "Death of a great Cricketer," and "Death of Victor Trumper" were on all the London placards instead of the sequence of war sensations.

It is very doubtful if there has ever been a greater batsman than Trumper, and his wonderful deeds would have been even greater but for indifferent health, which, in the end, cut short his life.

No one ever played so naturally, and he was as modest as he was magnificent. To this day in Australia, he is regarded as the highest ideal of batsmanship. He was, I think, the most fascinating batsman I have ever seen. He had grace, ease, style, and power, and a quickness of foot both in jumping out and in getting back to a ball that can surely never be surpassed.

He had every known stroke, and one or two of his own, and when set on a good wicket it seemed impossible to place the field for him. He was somewhat slightly built, but his sense of timing was so perfect that he hit the ball with tremendous power. Most bowlers are agreed that he was the most difficult batsman to keep quiet. I have heard a great bowler remark, "I could, in the ordinary way, keep most people from scoring quickly, but I always felt rather helpless against Trumper, for he was so quick, and he had so many strokes."

Whenever I think of him, my mind goes back to December 1903, and to the Sydney Cricket Ground. England had a lead of 292 runs on the first innings, and three Australians were out for something like 100 runs. The position was rather desperate from an Australian point of view, when Trumper's lithe and graceful figure appeared, accompanied by the tremendous cheering that can come from an Australian crowd. Here was their idol, their hero; here was the man who, with all his magnificent greatness, was always charming and pleasant and modest, and here was one who was going to put things right—and he did. He played gloriously, was undefeated at the end of the innings, and Australia nearly won the match.

In the heyday of his power, Trumper had as partner R. A. Duff, a brilliant attacking batsman, and when these two were seen coming out to open the innings for New South Wales or for Australia, the crowd used to rub their hands and say, " Here they come, Trumper and Duff," as, in later years, they paid the same tribute to Hobbs and Rhodes.

Trumper's best season in England was 1902, a *very wet summer*, and his play in that year is one of the monuments of cricket. He scored 2,570 runs and made eleven centuries. The state of the wicket made little difference to him, and his brilliant batting stirred cricketing England. His unrivalled skill and resource will never be forgotten. Before that, in his first Test Match at Lord's, in 1899, he had scored 135 not out, and, as Mr. Altham says in his splendid book *The History of Cricket*, " Before he had batted for half an hour, it was obvious that a new star of unsurpassed brilliance and charm had joined the cluster of the Southern course."

It may be interesting to recall that the first googly B. J. T. Bosanquet sent down to Trumper clean bowled him. The occasion was the match between Lord Hawke's XI and New South Wales, at Sydney, in March 1903.

SOME PERSONALITIES OF THE GAME

Trumper and Duff had gone in first in the New South Wales second innings and in thirty-five minutes had scored 72 runs by batting, every stroke of which I remember vividly to this day. Bosanquet went on to bowl, and his first ball pitched a good length just outside the off stump. Trumper thought it was a leg-break, and proceeded to cut it, late, as he hoped, for 4, but it came back and down went his off stump. Subsequently, he used to " murder " Bosanquet, but it is worth recording that the first " googly " ever bowled in Australia bowled out the man who, in spite of all the deeds of Don Bradman, many Australians still regard as the finest batsman their country has ever produced.

Trumper was also a magnificent deep field with a fine return, and he could throw a cricket ball over 100 yards. When he died the whole of Australia mourned him, and at his funeral the streets of Sydney were lined five and six deep. He was carried to his grave by eleven Australian players. No cricketer was ever more popular, and he deserved it, for he preserved the modesty of true greatness and was the beau-ideal of a cricketer.

III

TOM RICHARDSON

English cricket was rich in fast bowling in the 'nineties, and early years of this century. Every county had a fast bowler, some two—Surrey, for instance, the renowned Richardson and Lockwood.

Richardson was a man of giant build, with a great shock of black hair, the heart of a lion, and a high, impressive action. He loved bowling, " but never did he use his great pace to intimidate, and often and often he would handicap himself by moderating his speed, or bowling on the off-side when the wicket was dangerous, or when he had inadvertently hit a batsman. No day was too long for him, no sun too hot, no cause too desperate." I quote from Major H. S. Altham's *History of Cricket,* a book which is too little known, and which every lover of cricket should make a point of reading.

Richardson was at his best between 1894 and 1897, and in these four years he captured 1,005 wickets in first-class cricket in England for 14 runs apiece. It is, I think, correct to say that Lockwood, at his best, was a finer fast bowler than Richardson, but, day in, day out, for sheer consistency and concentrated excellence, Richardson could bear comparison with any fast bowler that ever lived ; and it was a stirring and inspiring sight to see these two men striving to win a match for Surrey on a hard, true wicket at The Oval.

Richardson obtained most of his wickets by pace, combined with an off-break that was achieved as much by body swing as by finger spin. On the best of wickets he could bring the ball back at a tremendous pace, and though I have heard it suggested that the modern batsman, padded to the thigh with his enormously big pads, which incidentally must affect his quickness of foot, would have lessened the number of his wickets, I do not think that they would have played him deliberately with the legs. At all events, I fancy they would have used the bat as well, for a blow from him certainly did hurt ; but such was the genial and happy spirit of the man that he invariably apologised when one of these superb break-backs hit one inside the right thigh.

Richardson could also bowl an extremely good yorker, and, naturally, with his height and pace he could make a good-length ball get up, and many a man has been caught at the wicket, or in the slips, off him.

Many great feats stand to his name, but the greatest of all was at Old Trafford in the England and Australia Match of 1896. Australia were set 125 runs to make to win. They lost four for 45, and seven for 100, and then

SOME PERSONALITIES OF THE GAME

H. Trumble and J. J. Kelly took an hour to get the last 25. In the whole match, Richardson bowled 110 overs, and obtained thirteen wickets, and in the second innings of the Australians he bowled for *three hours without a rest*, sending down 42 overs of 5 balls each, and taking six wickets for 72 runs. Never in the history of cricket has there been a finer example of stamina, accuracy, and sustained pace. For three mortal hours by the clock he put his whole soul into every ball he bowled, and if ever a man deserved to win a victory for his side, Richardson did on that occasion. This bowling of his in the second innings is, and I think always will be, quoted as a supreme example of concentrated determination, and of the spirit that never will acknowledge defeat until the last ball has been bowled and the umpires are removing the bails.

Richardson went twice to Australia, and bowled very well there. He was " pasted " by those two great, left-handed batsmen, Clem Hill and Joe Darling, on his second tour, but he won the rubber for Mr. Stoddart in 1894, and amongst the great bowlers of the world his fame is everlasting.

Richardson and Lockwood were the stars of a group of remarkable fast bowlers. Apart from them, there were Mold and W. Brearley, of Lancashire, a little later N. A. Knox, of Surrey, C. J. Kortright, Young, and Buckingham, of Essex, W. M. Bradley and Fielder, of Kent, Braund, of Sussex, Field, of Warwickshire, Wilson and Burrows, of Worcestershire, J. T. Brown, Junior, of Yorkshire, Warren and Bestwick, of Derbyshire, Woodcock, of Leicestershire, G. L. Jessop, of Gloucestershire, S. M. J. Woods and Gill, of Somerset. Moreover, Australia had E. Jones and A. Cotter, and South Africa J. J. Kotze. I think Kortright was the actual fastest of all these bowlers with Kotze *proxime accessit*. A batsman in those days had little chance of success if he could not play fast bowling.

CHAPTER FOURTEEN
Cricket in Prose and Verse
BY THOMAS MOULT

CHAPTER FOURTEEN

Cricket in Prose and Verse

BY THOMAS MOULT

THE game of cricket has been defined by one of its writers as, like summer itself, " the perfume and suppliance of a moment and no more." But surely the valiant deeds of the chosen champions of England and Australia, or South Africa and the other Test-match rivals, and the deeds, no less valiant though not regarded as quite so momentous, of the players in the county and club elevens, are sufficiently tangible to persist in the memory through many a moment, many a summer! Each player who holds the bat or ball has an opportunity to make something as enduring as most of what is written with the pen. No pen is needed for a team of cricketers to write a chapter as bright and thrilling, a passage as purple, as any to be found in the story-books. Out of the conflict and prowess of those companions in white may come a narrative so enthralling as to be comparatively immortal.

In literature itself, moreover, the authors who know their cricket (and some who don't) have shown that a moment's " perfume and suppliance " can be made to live on as long as the world of readers desires to share it. Poets, essayists, novelists: ever since—and long before—Charles Dickens took his Pickwickians gaily to witness the friendly struggle of the All-Muggletonians against the Dingley-Dellers in the days of long ago when cricketers played in top-hats and scored " notches " instead of runs, many have given their imagination to many a scene in which King Willow plays the principal part.

To review them, even without pretence of completeness, is to build up an anthology in little. Much that is in the vein of the Rev. Mr. Cotton's dithyrambic—

> 'Tis Cricket I sing, of illustrious fame,
> No nation e'er boasted so noble a game—

dated " Winchester, *circa* 1780," can be legitimately ignored in a chapter purporting to deal with the literature of cricket, not its curiosities. And it is safe to say that of the writings with any claim to be mentioned, *Cricket : an Heroic Poem*, by James Love, is entitled to first place chronologically. It describes in a style that has been called classically Johnsonian the match played between Kent and England on the Artillery Ground, London, on June 18th, 1744, to which reference has been made in an earlier chapter as the first of which the individual scores have been preserved. The poem was published in the same year, although the edition is undated and anonymous, and it was dedicated to the 4th Earl of Sandwich. Another edition followed in 1754, this time from Edinburgh instead of London, and it was accompanied by other pieces, the whole being entitled *Poems on Several Occasions*, James Love's name now appearing on the title-page. The third edition, sixteen years later, was announced as :

" *Cricket. An Heroic Poem* : Illustrated with the Critical Observations of Scriblerus Maximus. To which is added An Epilogue, call'd Bucks Have At Ye All. Spoken by Mr. King, at the Theatre Royal in Dublin, in the Character of Ranger, in *The Suspicious Husband*. By James Love, Comedian. London : Printed for the Author MDCCLXX. (Price One Shilling.)"

The dedication this time is " to the Members of the Cricket Club at Richmond in Surrey," in the hope that,

CRICKET IN PROSE AND VERSE

" founded upon Fact," it may " serve to entertain the true Lovers of Cricket, by a Recollection of many Particulars, at a time when the Game was cultivated with the utmost Assiduity, and patroniz'd by the personal Appearance and Management of some of the most capital People in the Kingdom." And entertain them it must have done, without a doubt. For after an opening invocation to the " tender Muse " of cricket, it becomes sufficiently rhapsodic to satisfy the most forthright fanatic :

> Hail, Cricket ! glorious, manly, British Game !
> First of all Sports ! be first alike in Fame !
> To my fir'd Soul thy busy transports bring
> That I may feel thy Raptures, while I sing. . . .
> Look round the Globe, inclin'd to Mirth, and see
> What daring Sport can claim the Prize from thee !
>
> Not puny Billiards, where with sluggish Pace
> The dull Ball trails before the feeble Mace.
> Where no triumphant shouts, no clamours dare
> Pierce thro' the vaulted Roof and wound the Air.
> But stiff Spectators quite inactive stand
> Speechless, attending to the Striker's Hand :
> Where nothing can your languid Spirits move,
> Save when the Marker bellows out Six love ! . . .
> Nor yet that happier game, where the smooth Bowl,
> In circling Mazes, wanders to the Goal ;
> Where, much divided between Fear and Glee,
> The Youth cries Rub : O Flee, You Ling'rer, Flee !
>
> Not Tennis self, thy sister sport, can charm,
> Or with thy fierce Delights our Bosoms warm.
> Tho' full of Life, at Ease alone dismay'd,
> She calls each swelling Sinew to her Aid.
> Her echoing Courts confess the sprightly Sound
> While from the Racket the brisk Balls rebound.
> Yet, to small Space confined, ev'n she must yield
> To nobler CRICKET the disputed Field.

BAT AND BALL

Britain is implored to beware of " sloth-promoting sports," " Eunuch Sports " :

> Shun with Disdain the squeaking Masquerade,
> Where fainting Vice calls Folly to her Aid.
> Leave the dissolving Song, the baby Dance
> To soothe the Slaves of Italy and France.

The match and its heroes are grandiloquently described : until the Kent Champion " strikes " and sends a catch to one who, though tumbling as he makes it, " glorious in his Fall, with Arm extended shows the captive Ball." And—

> The last two Champions even now are in,
> And but three Notches yet remain to win.
> When, almost ready to recant its Boast,
> Ambitious Kent within an Ace has lost :
> The mounting Ball, again obliquely driven,
> Cuts the pure Aether, soaring up to Heaven.
> W——k was ready : W——k all must own,
> As sure a swain to catch as e'er was known ;
> Yet, whether Jove, and all-compelling Fate,
> In their high Will determin'd Kent should beat ;
> Or the lamented Youth too much relied
> On sure Success, and Fortune often tried,
> The erring Ball, amazing to be told !
> Slip'd thro' his outstretch'd Hand, and mock'd his Hold.

So, because of " Butterfingers," the sons of Kent complete the game with a victory, " and firmly fix their everlasting Fame."

In this poem, incidentally, the terms " seekers-out " and " watchers-out " are used. They became obsolete long ago, as F. S. Ashley-Cooper points out, but Gilbert White, the classic author of *Selborne,* uses them as a matter of course in 1786, when, writing to his nephew, he states that " little Tom Clement is visiting at Petersfield, where he plays much at cricket: Tom bats: his grandmother bowls: and his great-grandmother watches out!!!" Another incidental comment on James Love's poem that may usefully be made is that it had for its sequel an astonishing piece of plagiarism. A portion of the poem appeared in the *Sporting Magazine* for May 1803, the name of Newland being omitted from the list of players and that of Lord F. Beauclerk used instead. It was also dedicated to Lord Frederick by the pretending author, who signed himself " J. J. B."

There are many references to cricket in classic literature before Love, such as that in Lord Chesterfield's letters to his son—" If you have a right ambition you will desire to excell all boys of your age at cricket . . . as well as in learning "—reminding us of Lord Byron's in *Hours of Idleness*—"together joined in cricket's manly toil"; Byron, who played for Harrow versus Eton. . . . But all such references are slight; and then we come to the anonymous narrative in verse describing a great match played between the Earl of Tankerville's men and the Duke of Dorset's on Bourn-Paddock, rounded off with :

> God save the King and bless the land
> With plenty and increase ;
> And grant henceforth that idle games
> In harvest-time may cease.

Rules and Instructions for Playing at the Game of Cricket were issued in the same period, by T. Boxall. They included this piece of advice to a bowler " to Twist the Ball " :

" Make a white mark on the ball, and it is very easy for a young player to understand that a ball cannot go out of the hand without rolling round. By tossing a ball across a room so as to hit the ground only once, then when it rises from the ground he will discover whether it twists to the right or to the left, or whether it rolls straight forward :

for although the ball is tossed straight to a mark, yet it must not roll straight, if it does it will not twist after it hits the ground. When the ball goes out of a bowler's hand he must endeavour to make it twist a little across, then after it hits the ground it will twist the same way as it rolls when it goes from the hand; it is not done altogether by the twist of the hand, for whatever part of the hand or finger it touches last when it leaves the hand it will twist or roll directly from that part or place." . . .

This is soon succeeded by Mary Mitford's tribute to pastoral cricket in *Our Village*.

"I doubt if there be any scene in the world more animating or delightful than a cricket match—I do not mean a set match at Lord's Ground for money, hard money, between a certain number of gentlemen and players, as they are called—people who make a trade of that noble sport and degrade it into an affair of bettings and hedgings and cheatings, it may be, like boxing or horse-racing; nor do I mean a pretty fête in a gentleman's park, where one club of cricketing dandies encounter another such club, and where they show off in graceful costume to a gay marquee of admiring belles, who condescend so to purchase admiration, and while away a long morning in partaking cold collations, conversing occasionally, and seeming to understand the game—the whole being conducted according to ball-room etiquette, so as to be exceedingly elegant and exceedingly dull. No! the cricket that I mean is a real solid old-fashioned match between neighbouring parishes, where each attacks the other for honour and a supper, glory and half a crown a man. If there be any gentleman amongst them it is well—if not, it is so much the better."

In *Our Village* there is a charming story entitled "Lost and Won." It tells of the country love of Paul Holton, a local bowler of fame, and Letty Dale:

" Perhaps Letty had never looked so pretty in her life as at that moment. She was simply drest, as became her fallen fortunes. Her complexion was still coloured, like the apple blossom, with vivid red and white, but there was more of sensibility, more of the heart in its quivering mutability, its alternation of paleness and blushes; the blue eyes were still as bright, but they were oftener cast down : the smile was still as splendid, but far more rare : the girlish gaiety was gone, but it was replaced by womanly sweetness—sweetness and modesty formed now the chief expression of that lovely face, lovelier, far lovelier, than ever."

As for Paul, no wonder he " gazed and gazed with his whole soul in his eyes, in complete oblivion of cricket and cricketer, and the whole world ! " He had lost Letty through a misunderstanding three years earlier, but now he vowed to win her back—through his cricket. Off the field, of course, he was shy :

" He recollected himself, blushed and bowed, and advanced a few steps, as if to address her ; but, timid and irresolute, he turned away without speaking, joined the party who had now assembled round the wickets, the umpires called ' Play ' ! and the game began."

But on the field the story was a very different one. Indeed, Paul won the game for his side—and with his bat at that !

" All eyes were fixed on the Sussex cricketer, and at first he seemed likely to verify the prediction and confirm the hopes of the most malicious of his adversaries, by batting as badly as he had bowled well. He had not caught sight of the ball ; his hits were weak ; his defence insecure, and his mates began to tremble and his opponents to crow. Every hit seemed likely to be the last ; he missed a leg ball of Ned Smith's ; was all but caught out by Sam Newton ; and East Woodhay triumphed and Hazelby sat quaking, when a sudden glimpse of Letty, watching him with manifest anxiety, recalled her champion's wandering thoughts. Gathering himself up, he stood before the wicket another man; knocked the ball hither and thither, to the turnpike, the coppice, the pond; got three, four, five at a hit; baffled the slow bowler, James Smith, and the fast bowler, Tom Taylor; got fifty-five notches off his own bat; stood out all the rest of his side; and so handled the adverse party when they went in that the match was won at a single innings, with six-and-thirty runs to spare."

The victorious batsman thereupon approaches Letty Dale again, " and this time she did not run away. ' Letty, dear Letty,' said he, ' three years ago I lost the cricket match, and you were angry, and I was a fool. But Letty, dear Letty, this match is won, and if you could but know how deeply I have repented, how earnestly I have longed for this day.' " What else he said need not be quoted here, nor what she answered him. All that is necessary is to say that a month later the wedding bells " were ringing merrily in honour of one of the fairest and luckiest matches that ever cricketer lost and won."

Miss Mitford, of whom it ought to be recorded that she is the only author who ever struck lucky in a sweepstake, for at the age of ten she won £20,000, wrote a good deal about cricket. In the same volume she describes with great gusto the ups and downs of an afternoon on the field. " William Grey made a hit which actually lost the cricket-ball. We think she lodged in a hedge, a quarter of a mile off, but nobody could find her. And George Simmons had nearly lost his shoe, which he tossed away in a passion, for having been caught out, owing to the ball glancing against it. These, together with a very complete somersault of Ben Appleton, our long-stop, who floundered about in the mud, making faces and attitudes as laughable as Grimaldi, none could tell whether by accident or design, were the chief incidents of the action. Among the spectators nothing remarkable occurred, beyond the great calamity of two or three drenchings, except that a form, placed by the side of a hedge, under a very insufficient shelter, was knocked into the ditch, in a sudden rush of the cricketers to escape a pelting shower, by which means all parties shared the fate of Ben Appleton, some on land and some by water; and that, amidst the scramble, a saucy gipsy of a girl contrived to steal from the knee of the demure and well-apparelled Samuel Long, a smart handkerchief which his careful dame had tied round it to preserve his new (what is the mincing feminine word?)—his new—inexpressibles, thus reversing the story of Desdemona, and causing the new Othello to call aloud for his handkerchief, to the great diversion of the company. And so we parted; the players retired to their supper, and we to our homes; all wet through, all good-humoured and happy—except the losers."

Another Mitford was Mary's contemporary, John Mitford, who eulogised a parson-batsman so wholeheartedly in the *Gentleman's Magazine* that he even went so far as to ask that, with his " black, unhooded head, his red, shining face, and his all but shirtless body," he might be secured " the living of St. John's Wood where he could play and preach alternately." But John Mitford's best though rather florid writing is to be found in his comparisons among sports and pastimes :

" All the Nations in Europe are in some sense sportsmen; the cry of the hound, and the horn of the huntsman, is heard from the Grampian Hills to the very granite steeps of Hæmus. The hare is coursed alike on the downs of Swaffham and the arid plains of Ispahan; and the sound of the fatal and unerring rifle breaks the repose equally of the woods of Lochabar and the distant forests of Tiflis.

"On the other hand, there are many pursuits and games which are confined within certain limits, and belong to a peculiar people. Tennis used to be the favourite pastime of the French: shooting at the wooden bird of the Swiss. Balone is the magnificent and splendid diversion of the Italian nobles. Skating is the Dutchman's pleasure. And thus Cricket is the pride and the privilege of the Englishman alone. Into this, his noble and favourite amusement, no other people ever pretended to penetrate; a Frenchman or German would not know which end of a bat they were to hold; and so fine, so scientific, and so elaborate is the skill regarding it that only a small part of England have as yet acquired a knowledge of it. In this Kent has always stood proudly pre-eminent; Kent is emphatically the field of the cricketer's glory."

There is also Mitford's grand valedictory to the scenes he had known, the heroes he had adored. "Farewell, ye smiling fields of Hambledon and Windmill Hill! Farewell, ye thymy pastures of our beloved Hampshire, and farewell, ye spirits of the brave who still hover over the fields of your inheritance. Great and illustrious eleven! fare ye well! in these fleeting pages at least, your names shall be enrolled. What would life be, deprived of the recollection of you? Troy has fallen, and Thebes is a ruin. The pride of Athens is decayed and Rome is crumbling to the dust. The philosophy of Bacon is wearing out; and the victories of Marlborough have been overshadowed by fresher laurels. All is vanity but CRICKET; all is sinking in oblivion but you. Greatest of all elevens, fare ye well!"

But the Mitfords and all the other writers about cricket in the early nineteenth century were merely—we use the term without belittlement—the forerunners of one about whom Andrew Lang wrote that "if Love were the Homer of cricket, the minstrel who won from forgetfulness the glories of the dim Heroic Age, Nyren was the delightful Herodotus of the early Historic Period." John Nyren is the author of—or, rather, to him is attributed, though Charles Cowden Clarke obviously wrote—*The Young Cricketer's Tutor*: to which is added *The Cricketers of My Time*.

How much of this great little classic of cricket can be called John Nyren's, and how much his " ghost's " ? For if Nyren is to be regarded as one of the few who have produced anything in cricket that can be called literature, then surely Clarke is another. We are not prepared, however, to dispute the pre-eminent position of Nyren. If Clarke wrote down Nyren's thoughts and opinions in the style he estimated Nyren would adopt had he used the pen himself, then *The Young Cricketer's Tutor* has the right name on its title-page as long as it has the other partner's name there also.

Nyren's book is a triumphant proof of how beauty and utility may go together. In the middle of severely practical dissertations we come upon such a passage as that which describes " Sir Horace Mann, walking about, outside the ground, cutting down the daisies with his stick—a habit with him when he was agitated : the old farmers leaning forward upon their tall old staves, and the whole multitude perfectly still " ; or that with which an analysis of George Lear's skill as the Hambledon " long-stop " is concluded : " Lear was a short man, of a fair complexion, well-looking, and of a pleasing aspect. He had a sweet counter tenor voice. Many a treat have I had in hearing him and Sueter join in a glee at the ' Bat and Ball ' on Broad Halfpenny :

> I have been there, and still would go ;
> 'Twas like a little Heaven below ! "

BAT AND BALL

Love of the game and all that it involves—combat and companionship, the sunlight mood and a certain picturesqueness—are manifested in every page. The best is that in which we get the fine phrase, " Go hard ! *Tich* and turn ! *Tich* and turn." It is well-known, but, like all classic writing, it stands any amount of repetition :

"There was high feasting held on Broad Halfpenny during the solemnity of one of our grand matches. Oh ! it was a heart-stirring sight to witness the multitude forming a complete and dense circle round that noble green. Half the country would be present, and all their hearts with us. Little Hambledon pitted against All England was a proud thought for the Hambledon men. Defeat was glory in such a struggle—Victory, indeed, made us only ' a little lower than angels.' How these fine, brown-faced fellows of farmers would drink to our success ! And then what stuff they had to drink ! Punch !—not your new *Ponche à la Romaine* or *Ponche à la Groseille*, or your modern cat-lap milk punch—punch bedevilled ; but good, unsophisticated John Bull stuff—stark !—that would stand on end—punch that would make a cat speak ! Sixpence a bottle ! We had not sixty millions of interest to pay in those days. The ale too !—not the modern horror under the same name, that drives as many men melancholy-mad as the hypocrites do ; not the beastliness of these days, that will make a fellow's inside like a shaking bog—and as rotten ; but barleycorn, such as would put the souls of three butchers into one weaver. Ale that would flare like turpentine—genuine Boniface ! This immortal viand (for it was more than liquor) was vended at twopence per pint. The immeasurable villainy of our vintners would, with their march of intellect (if ever they could get such a brewing), drive a pint of it out into a gallon. Then the quantities the fellows would eat ! Two or three of them would strike dismay into a round of beef. They could no

CRICKET IN PROSE AND VERSE

more have pecked in that style than they could have flown, had the infernal black stream (that type of Acheron!) which soddens the carcass of a Londoner, been the fertiliser of their clay.

"There would this company, consisting most likely of some thousands, remain patiently and anxiously watching every turn of fate in the game, as if the event had been the meeting of two armies to decide their liberty. And whenever a Hambledon man made a good hit, worth four or five runs, you would hear the deep mouths of the whole multitude baying away in pure Hampshire, ' Go hard ! Go hard ! *Tich* and turn ! *Tich* and turn ! ' To the honour of my countrymen, let me bear testimony upon this occasion also, as I have already done upon others. Although their provinciality in general, and personal partialities individually, were naturally interested in behalf of the Hambledon men, I cannot call to recollection an instance of their wilfully stopping a ball that had been hit out among them by one of our opponents. Like *true* Englishmen, they would give an enemy fair play. How strongly are all those scenes, of fifty years bygone, painted in my memory ! —and the smell of that ale comes as freshly upon me as the new May flowers."

There was much contemporary writing by others in the spirit of Nyren's *Young Cricketer's Tutor*. Philip Norman's *Annals of the West Kent Cricket Club* includes a worthily preserved dialect song called " The Kentish Cricketer," written, we are told, " long before railroads, board schools, etc., had begun to smooth away the local peculiarities of country life." In this song a yokel describes his visit to London, where he finds himself " on my Lord's cricket ground." There he stood " hankerin' about," and " Well, Sir, my Lord he cum up to me and axed me if I cud play any or nay. ' I doan't know, my Lord,' I ses, ses I. ' I bean't no gurt spaiks of a player ; mine's an aukerdish kind of a knock, a sort of a lapper right round de field !' 'Well, my man,' ses he, 'can ye boal?' 'Aha, my Lord, Sir,' I ses, 'I jest can; I always het de man or de wicket to a dead sartinty.'

> Well, my Lord then ses he, ' Yu're de man jest for me,'
>   Tol de rol de rol lol de rol li do.
>
> We shartly strip'd in, and de geam did begin,
>   An' at fust it went on pretty rightish;
> Till we'd been in twice, an' it looked rather queer,
>   For they knock'd her about pretty tightish,
> 'Bout losing de geam, we thought one an' all;
>   When my Lord ses to me, ' Cannot you take the ball ?'

" And be darned if I didn't too, and a teejous good boul I made on it, for I broke so many heads, arms, legs, bats, and wickets, de geam was nation soon our'n.

> An' t'other chaps then were all hospital men,
>   Tol de rol de rol lol de rol li do."

In *Peter Parley's Annual*, 1840, we are informed that: " Cricket is a noble game. Why, do you know that even blood royal has stood, bat in hand, surrounded by the young buds of nobility; and I can tell you this, that the Prince of Wales, afterwards George the Fourth, was a noble cricketer, and few could bowl him out." The writer proceeds to tell an anecdote of Prince George which occurred when he was a cricketer and, incidentally, is additional evidence that violent bowling is not an exclusive product of the nineteen-thirties, as some people would have us believe. The Prince went disguised as a civilian to a match between Berkshire and Buckinghamshire, on which side was a little shoemaker " who, having a keen eye and strong arm, had acquired such extraordinary skill in bowling that few could defend a wicket against him."

CRICKET IN PROSE AND VERSE

"What bit of thing is that at the wicket?" asked the cobbler when the Prince went in to bat. "Oh, he is a tailor," said someone who stood by. "Then," said the bowler, "I'll break his bat for him." Whereupon he bowled "with amazing force and velocity": but the Prince "blocked it as dead as a stone." The shoemaker held his hands over his eyes and surveyed the Prince from top to bottom. "No tailor could do that," he said; "he must be a lad of wax." And when somebody agreed, he went on, "Then I will melt him before I have done with him." In vain, though, until he summoned up his energy "for one grand effort." "He went back for a considerable distance, took an exact aim, ran with all his force to the popping crease, and delivered—how? As gently as the thistledown flies along the air: the ball ran along the grass like a snake, and stopped just in the middle of the wicket, knocking off the cross piece like a fly." The Prince flung down his bat, "seemingly mortified"; nevertheless, he rewarded the cobbler with a heavy purse, and said: "if he makes shoes as well as he plays cricket, he shall be my shoemaker." The yarn concludes with the statement that "this bowler was shoemaker to the Prince and George the Fourth after he came to the throne."

Next to Nyren and the Mitfords, perhaps higher than the two last named as a writer who speaks with authority, is the Rev. James Pycroft, whose two volumes, *The Cricket Field* and *Cricketana*, were published in the early eighteen-fifties. Pycroft can write of those sunny hours "when the valleys laugh and sing," but he is usually less picturesque, more forthright, than Nyren (he had not the friend of Shelley, Leigh Hunt, and Charles Lamb behind him), and he may be described as a high-class pedestrian. Occasionally a passage in his works can be made to stand in splendid isolation:

"I never can walk about Lord's without some such

BAT AND BALL

reflections as may be supposed in Rip Van Winkle after his sleep of twenty years; the present and the past come in such vivid contrast before my mind. There is this peculiarity about Lord's as suggestive of such sobering reflections—in other haunts, as in the parks and fashionable promenades, the frequenters change—two or three seasons satisfy the many; but not so at Lord's. Once a cricketer, always a cricketer—as a looker-on, at least.

"Poor Felix died in 1880, in Dorsetshire, having survived his sad attack of paralysis nearly twenty years. I often tried, but never could prevail on him to take my arm, and even from the loop-hole of his retreat just to sit still with me, and to criticise and compare play present and past on those fields where once he had been the one man people came to see. 'No,' he said. 'Old recollections, and I fear old friends too, will crowd around; the gap is too wide, the fall is too great, it would upset me quite.'

"Yes, that ring at Lord's shows me every gradation in the scale of life—the once active now stiff and heavy, the youthful grey, the leaders of great elevens passing unrecognised and alone. Every old cricketer knows by sight, and is himself known to hundreds from frequenting Lord's—people who seem to him as distinct and as peculiar to those haunts as if he returned periodically to another land."

In another book Pycroft returns to Lord's. "Oh! that ring at Lord's," he exclaims; "for, as in olden time—

> Si quid fricti ciceris probat et nucis emptor;

that is, if the swillers of half-and-half and smokers of pigtail—a preponderating influence and a large majority of voices—applaud a hit, it does not follow that it is a good one, nor, if they cry 'Butterfingers!' need the miss be a bad one. No credit for good intentions! no allowance for a twisting catch, and the sun enough to singe your eyelids!

CRICKET IN PROSE AND VERSE

—the hit that wins the 'half-and-half' is the finest hit for that select assemblage, whose 'sweet voices' quite drown the nicer judgment of the pavilion, even as vote by ballot would swamp the House of Lords."

It is strange to have to speak of Charles Dickens as a lesser writer in any connection whatsoever, but that is what we are required to do in regard to his references to cricket. Even so, what delightful fun it is, his description in *The Pickwick Papers* of the match between All-Muggleton and Dingley Dell. " Several players were stationed to 'look out,' in different parts of the field, and each fixed himself into the proper attitude by placing one hand on each knee, and stooping very much as if he were 'making a back' for some beginner at leap-frog. All the regular players do this sort of thing : indeed it is generally supposed that it is quite impossible to look out properly in any other position. . . ." A fig for technical correctness ! . . . " The umpires were stationed behind the wickets : the scorers were prepared to notch the runs ; a breathless silence ensued. Mr. Luffey retired a few paces behind the wicket of the passive Podder, and applied the ball to his right eye for several seconds. Dumkins confidently awaited its coming, with his eyes fixed on the motions of Luffey. 'Play,' suddenly cried the bowler. . . ." Let it be remembered that Dickens wrote this as a contemporary of Nyren, and fifteen years before Pycroft. But even if his knowledge had been as great as theirs, he could not have bettered the staccato narrative of Mr. Jingle :

" ' Capital game—well played—some strokes admirable,' said the stranger, as both sides crowded into the tent, at the conclusion of the game.

" ' You have played it, sir ? ' inquired Mr. Wardle, who had been much amused by his loquacity.

" ' Played it ! Think I have—thousands of times—not here—West Indies—exciting thing—hot work—very.'

BAT AND BALL

" ' It must be rather a warm pursuit in such a climate,' observed Mr. Pickwick.

" ' Warm !—red-hot—scorching—glowing.—Played a match once—single wicket—friend the Colonel—Sir Thomas Blazo—who should get greatest number of runs.—Won the toss—first innings—seven o'clock, a.m.—six natives to look out—went in ; kept in—heat intense—natives all fainted—taken away—fresh half-dozen ordered—fainted also—Blazo bowling—supported by two natives—couldn't bowl me out—fainted too—cleared away Colonel—wouldn't give in—faithful attendant—Quanko Samba—last man left—sun so hot, bat in blisters, ball scorched brown—five hundred and seventy runs—rather exhausted—Quanko mustered up last remaining strength—bowled me out—had a bath, and went out to dinner.'

" ' And what became of What's-his-name, sir ? ' inquired an old gentleman.

" ' Blazo ? '

" ' No—the other gentleman.'

" ' Quanko Samba ? '

" ' Yes, sir.'

" ' Poor Quanko—never recovered it—bowled on, on my account—bowled off, on his own—died, sir ! ' Here the stranger buried his countenance in a brown jug, but whether to hide his emotion or imbibe its contents, we cannot distinctly affirm. We only know that he paused suddenly, drew a long and deep breath, and looked anxiously on, as two of the principal members of the Dingley Dell club approached Mr. Pickwick, and said—

" ' We are about to partake of a plain dinner at the Blue Lion, sir ; we hope you and your friends will join us.'

" ' Of course,' said Mr. Wardle, ' among our friends we include Mr. —— ' ; and he looked towards the stranger.

" ' Jingle,' said that versatile gentleman, taking the hint

at once. 'Jingle—Alfred Jingle, Esq., of No Hall, Nowhere.'"

Dickens (after Miss Mitford) did not exactly set a fashion of cricket in fiction when he introduced it into *The Pickwick Papers*. As a matter of fact, never again in all his novels was he to mention the game at such a length, and it was not until George Meredith appeared some twenty years later that we read about an imaginary cricket match. In *The Adventures of Harry Richmond*, an omnibus-driver informed Harry and his friends " that he had backed the Surrey eleven . . . owing to the report of a gentleman-bowler, who had done things in the way of tumbling wickets to tickle the ears of cricketers." Then, as a prelude to the talk between Harry and his friend " of the ancient raptures of a first of May cricketing-day on a sunny green meadow, with an ocean of a day before us, and well-braced spirits for the match," the driver delivers a fine homily. " I asks why don't more gentlemen take to cricket ? 'stead of horses all the year round !" This man, " condemned to inactivity, in the perpetual act of motion," declared cricket to be his notion of happiness—" cricket in cricket season ! It comprises—count : lots o' running ; and that's good : just enough o' taking it easy ; that's good ; a appetite for your dinner, and your ale or your port, as may be the case ; good, number three. Add on a tired pipe after dark, and a sound sleep to follow, and you say good morning to the doctor and the parson ; for you're in health body and soul, and ne'er a parson'll make a better Christian o' ye, that I'll swear."

George Meredith writes about cricket in three other novels—*Evan Harrington, Diana of the Crossways*, and *The Ordeal of Richard Feverel*. One game he describes as full of " grand spanking hits " and bowling feats galore. Tom Redworth, in *Diana of the Crossways*, bats in a flannel jacket and black trousers, a peculiar combination even in those days, and there was a fieldsman called the "long-hit-off." One of Meredith's contemporaries, Anthony Trollope, introduces a match into his little-known romance *The Fixed Period* that is truly leviathan—"England *v.* Brittanula." But in describing this astonishing game Trollope was having a little fun with his readers, for he blandly informs us that the match was played in the year 1980!

By way of extenuation in the case of Dickens and Trollope, and to some degree George Meredith, it must be said that they had not the advantage of reading up all our modern experts before they wrote their chapters. But, then, neither had Miss Mitford, a mere lady; not only did she put these three fellow-novelists to shame, but Thomas Hughes also—Thomas Hughes especially, for the author of *Tom Brown's Schooldays* was deadly serious, and yet his boys are made to do some extraordinary things. A certain Jack Ruggles, who has a prejudice against wearing pads and gloves, made a hit to leg for five from a ball pitched on the off. Another batsman made "a forward drive," and "the cover-point hitter, that cunning man, goes on to bowl slow twisters." After luncheon the rival teams engaged in "topping comic songs," a dreadful innovation which, as one critic suggested, possibly led to the match being left unfinished. None of Tom Brown's comrades on the cricket field seems to be particularly modest: between overs, for instance, "Jack walks swaggering about his wicket, with the bat over his shoulder." Also he "waves his hand triumphantly towards the tent, as much as to say, 'See if I don't finish it all off now in three hits.'"

Many a modern novelist has included cricket and cricketers in his plot. Mr. Hugh de Sélincourt made an entire novel, *The Cricket Match*, out of a Saturday game in a village, and he was so successful that it thoroughly deserved Sir James Barrie's tribute—" the best that has ever been written about cricket or any other game." The novel is as simple as the idea of cricket itself. Dawn breaks over the village of Tillingfold. In their various homes, cottage and villa and mansion, the cricketers wake up, pass the morning, and assemble on the field and play their match. Then they disperse: " Gauvinier mounted his bicycle and rode home into the glory of the evening. Even the cricket match was forgotten for a little while as he looked at the blaze of colour which celebrated the close of the day. He rode slowly, lingering as at a majestic rite. The whole vast sky glowed red and orange; the trees shone rosy in the reflected light which touched the hills. No breath of wind stirred the glowing stillness. His heart worshipped God and colour and life. And night was treading softly from the woods where the little owls were beginning to cry. . . . Rich and poor, old and young, were seeking sleep."

To say that Mr. de Sélincourt has excelled all other novelists is not to refuse acknowledgment of Mr. C. B. Fry's *Mother and Son*, in which we follow a cricketer's progress from crude boyhood to batting gianthood, or Mr. J. C. Snaith's *Willow the King!* E. W. Hornung's delightful scoundrel Raffles performs notably as a bowler for Gentlemen *v.* Players at a country-house party, Mr. Horace Annesley Vachell introduced a memorable Eton and Harrow match into his school story *The Hill*, Mr. P. G. Wodehouse (before the Jeeves era) made cricket a remarkably serious matter in several stories, and Mr. Eric Parker, in his beautiful and delicate *Playing Fields*, immortalised (among other features) one version of the old wet-weather pastime of " paper cricket ":

" In the dining-room the oak panels and the deep bays of the windows wore a pleasant air of comfort. Martin glanced at the rain dripping from the filbert trees in the garden. Ibbetson and he were soon deep in comparison of dates and colours of stamps. Torr and Bincastle, of the fourth class, were playing a game of cricket on paper. You wrote down the names of two elevens on two sheets of paper and then dotted a pencil with your eyes shut on another piece of paper, which was marked with 'fourers,' 'sixers,' 'caught,' 'bowled,' and so on.

" ' That's another six to W. G. By Jove, he is hitting. That's seven out of the ground now. That makes him 202.'

" ' Bet he'll soon be bowled, then.'

" ' Bet he isn't.'

" ' There you are, then. Bowled, Spofforth. Told you so.'

" ' Well, he's made two hundred, anyhow. Spofforth's average must be simply rotten.'

" ' Ass ! He's only just gone on.'

" ' Why didn't you put him on before, then ? Just shows.' "

Paper cricket, incidentally, is (or was) also played with each letter of the alphabet representing a hit or an " out," and a page or column in a book or newspaper scrupulously followed. . . . Mr. Parker's novel also contains a chapter on an Eton *v.* Harrow match that is uncommonly rich in colour and movement ; an artist has painted Lord's cricket ground in words that glow and shimmer :

" The ground was emptying. At the gates cabs and carriages passed, drove up, drove off. Martin found himself in a group moving towards the gap opposite the entrance. Towards the gap marched a knot of dark-blue colours : a Harrow boy at its head, with a broken hat and a cut cheek.

" ' Harrow ! Harrow ! '

" A girl of fifteen, in grey silk, marched by the side. She brandished a dark-blue handkerchief tied on the end

CRICKET IN PROSE AND VERSE

of an umbrella. Her lips were parted, her grey eyes blazing.

" ' Harrow ! Harrow ! ' she shouted.

" She was hoarse. She waved her dark-blue banner. Joan of Arc ; the Maid. . . .

" The dark-blue banner swept on."

Sir James Barrie wrote deliciously in *The Little White Bird* about a cricket " match " between two boys to determine the sex of a new arrival in the family, expected any day : " If he won it was to be a girl, and if I won it was to be a boy." This is to be expected of one who has written two privately-printed booklets on the game as he played it—*Allahakbarries C.C. : 1893*, and *The Allahakbarrie Book of Broadway Cricket : 1899*. The author describes the players in his country-house team, including himself : " Barrie (Capt.). An Incomparable Captain. The life and soul of his side. A treat to see him tossing the penny. Hits well off his pads. Once took a wicket." The captain's hints include : " Should you hit the ball, run at once. Don't stop to cheer." One of the players is described as " the worst batsman in the world. Equally at home with the ball." There is also a description of a match. " The Captain received valuable help from Watson (who played a masterly innings of 2), from Whibley (who defied the best bowling in Shere for nearly a minute), from the hard-hitting Partridge (who would be invaluable against his own bowling), and from Tomson, who looked like scoring at any moment."

The references to cricket in Barrie's other writings are numerous, and in an equally droll vein. When Nell Meredith speaks disparagingly to Will Abinger about one of his friends, in *When a Man's Single*, that young hero-worshipper declares, with an air of giving an overwhelming rebuttal, that " he made a hundred and three against Rugby and was only bowled off his pads." Later on Will discovers that a famous explorer does not know what l.b.w. means, and although he could not despise a man who has shot lions, " he never had quite the same respect for the King of Beasts again." Then, towards the end of the same book, we hear of a great enthusiast who, having wooed Nell, " found that he had to give up either Nell or a cricket match, and so Nell was reluctantly dropped." In the play, *Walker, London,* Mr. Upjohn (who once made 121 for Middlesex *v.* Notts) is worshipped by a boy who calls himself " W. G.," " because he likes to fancy that he is a reincarnation of W. G. Grace, England's great nineteenth-century cricketer." (The eternal mind of the boy—how well Barrie knows it !—is in that brief stage-direction.) " I would rather take three wickets in an over," vows this " W. G.," " than be Shakespeare and Homer and all those swells put together."

Andrew Lang's cricket poetry might almost be described as rhymed Barrie :

> If the wild bowler thinks he bowls,
>   Or if the batsman thinks he's bowled,
> They know not, poor misguided souls—

the piece is entitled " Brahma (after Emerson) "—

> They both shall perish unconsoled.
> *I* am the batsman and the bat,
>   *I* am the bowler and the ball,
> The umpire, the pavilion cat,
>   The roller, pitch, and stumps, and all.

It was Lang who once declared (in his introduction to Richard Daft's *Kings of Cricket*) : " There is no talk, none so witty and brilliant, that is so good as cricket talk, when memory sharpens memory, and the dead live again—the regretted, the unforgotten—and the old happy days of burned-out Junes revive. We shall not see them again.

CRICKET IN PROSE AND VERSE

We lament that lost lightness of heart, 'for no man under the sun lives twice, outliving his day,' and the day of the cricketer is brief." That is hardly prose ; certainly it is near to Barrie. . . . Or, rather, Barrie is sometimes near to Lang ; near to him, for example, as he reveals his spirit in " Ballade of Dead Cricketers " :

> Ah, where be Beldham now, and Brett,
>   Barber, and Hogsflesh, where be they ?
> Brett, of all bowlers fleetest yet
>   That drove the bails in disarray ?
> And Small that would, like Orpheus, play
>   Till wild bulls followed his minstrelsy ? . . .
> And Richard Nyren, grave and grey ?
>   Beneath the daisies, there they lie !

The pathos of the game has for ever haunted its poets :

> All were proud of him, all loved him. As the changing seasons pass,
> As our champion lies a-sleeping underneath yon Kentish grass,
> Proudly, sadly, we will name him : to forget him were a sin ;
> Lightly lie the turf upon thee, kind and manly Alfred Mynn !

The elegy by William Jeffery Prowse, from which these lines are quoted, may almost be said to give modern cricket poetry its send-off. Soon afterwards William Barnes, the Dorset dialect-poet, makes one of his villagers say :

> I'll goo, an' we'll zet up a wicket,
> An' have a good innens at cricket ;

and then comes Francis Thompson, with the incomparable " Gloster Comes North " :

> It is little I repair to the matches of the Southron folk,
>   Though my own red roses there may blow ;
> It is little I repair to the matches of the Southron folk
>   Though the red roses crest the caps I know.

BAT AND BALL

> For the field is full of shades as I near the shadowy coast,
> And a ghostly batsman plays to the bowling of a ghost,
> And I look through my tears on a soundless clapping host,
>   As the run-stealers flicker to and fro,
>   To and fro.
>   O my Hornby and my Barlow long ago !

Not so familiar as this opening stanza, which is repeated as the culminating fourth, are the second and third, that recall " Gloster coming North, the irresistible, the Shire of the Graces, long ago ! " How, the poet asks, shall the " new-arisen Lancashire stand before all resistless Graces," whose bats are as maces ?—

> The long whiskered Doctor, that laugheth rules to scorn,
> While the bowler, pitched against him, bans the day that he was born ;
> And G. F. with his science makes the fairest length forlorn ;
>   They are come up from the West to work thee woe !

All-round as a man of letters, it is only to be expected that Mr. E. V. Lucas should have written cricket poems :

> Pour on us torrents of light, good Sun,
>   Shine in the hearts of my cricketers, shine ;
> Fill them with gladness and might, good Sun,
>   Touch them with glory, O Brother of mine,
>   Brother of mine,
>   Brother of mine !
> We are the lords of them, Brother and Mate ;
> I am a little ball, thou but a Great !

" The Cricket Ball Sings " is included in *Willow and Leather*, a volume published in 1899. So is " Driving to the Match "—

> The hoofs are on the road, boys,
>   They ring a merry catch,
> O the sun's at noon, and the year's at June,
>   And we're driving to the match—

CRICKET IN PROSE AND VERSE

in which is preserved the spirit of the old wagonette days, when " all the world is O so fair as we go driving by " ; and also " Good Days " :

> Willow and cane, nothing but that—
> O, but it's glorious, swinging the bat !
> Leather and thread, there you have all—
> O, but it's glorious, gripping the ball !
> Grass at our feet, and the sun overhead,
> Here let us play till the evening is red.
> Then to our dinner, and lustily sing,
> Cricket's the King of games, Cricket is King !

Edward Cracroft Lefroy, who died so long since as 1891, wrote a sonnet on "The Bowler" that still bears quotation :

> The flung ball takes one maddening, tortuous bound,
> And the mid-stump three somersaults in the air.

Sir Henry Newbolt makes a reference to school cricket in " Vitai Lampada " —

> There's a breathless hush in the Close to-night,
> Ten to make and the match to win—
> A bumping pitch and a blinding light
> An hour to play and the last man in.

A phrase, rather than the whole piece itself, is remembered in " The Proud Cricketer," by Harold Begbie :

England hath played at many a game, and ever her toy was a ball ;
But the meadow game, with the beautiful name, is king and lord of them all :
Cricket is King and lord of them all, thro' the sweet green English shires ;
And here's to the bat, and the ball (How's that ?), and the heart that never tires. . . .

BAT AND BALL

But when we are puffing through middle life, and it's time for the last sweet knocks,
When our average falls, and we fear fast balls, and the young 'uns call us crocks;
Well, watching the young 'uns play will serve, and still with our latest breath—
'Well played!' we'll shout from the ropes (Not out!)—and follow the game till death.

Begbie's contribution, of which these are the first and last of five verses, must nevertheless be ranked high in cricket poetry, which all too often is merely eulogy, or parody. . . . The laureate of the game has yet to come. So far the honour has been shared, and Mr. Alfred Cochrane, who played for Derbyshire, is among the sharers. Mr. Cochrane's *Collected Verses* and *Later Verses*, published in 1903 and 1918, are uncommonly happy; nor has he deserted the mood, for in 1927 he wrote "The Luck of the Toss (Rural Cricket in Derbyshire)," from which two verses are given:

It were long years back, in t'blacksmith's croft,
    As Jim an' I played cricket,
Wi' a bat an' a ball atwixt us both,
    An' a tree as stood for wicket.
We'd never a penny to toss for choice,
    So we'd chuck up t' bat, would we,
      'Ump!' says Jim,
      'Oller!' says I,
    An' 'Ump it is,' says 'e.

We was Test-match men, we was Durby-*shire*,
    An' wouldn't there come a shout
When Chatterton made a 'it for three,
    Or Docker were bowled for nowt!
When Jim were Spofforth, or summat o' that,
    An' I were W. G.
      'Ump!' says 'e,
      'Oller!' says I,
    An' 'Oller it is,' says 'e.

CRICKET IN PROSE AND VERSE

Mr. Cochrane has humour and poignancy as well as homeliness. Here is the " envoy " to " Ballade of the Corner Stroke " :

> Sirs, I was taken off ! expletives fail !
>   He never used the weapon's face at all ;
> They bowled him with an under like a snail—
>   This is the man who snicketh the length-ball.

And " England, Past and Present " begins :

> But for an hour to watch them play
>   Those heroes dead and gone,
> And pit our batsmen of to-day
>   With those of Hambledon !
> Our Graces, Nyrens, Studds, and Wards,
>   In weeks of sunny weather,
> Somewhere upon Elysian swards
>   To see them matched together !

Norman Gale, F. W. Harvey (" In the Slips "), G. F. Wilson, and G. D Martineau are also to be appreciated among the poets of cricket. Unfortunately, when poetry is mentioned to cricketers themselves—or, at any rate, to the average veteran—they think immediately and exclusively of " the humorous Craig," as a writer in *The Times Literary Supplement* refers to him, " who earned an honest living by peddling copies of his rough-and-ready verse at The Oval. He was not even an expert versifier : but he was a first-rate salesman. When a customer said to him : ' I could write verse as bad as this, Craig,' his ready retort : ' Yes, but could you sell it, Sir ? ' was rewarded by a general laugh and many pieces of silver, where coppers could only be expected."

We turn from the ridiculous to the sublime as we come to an author who is hard to classify—one of the few who, in an absolute sense, may be said to have enriched the *literature* of the game : Neville Cardus. Poet or prose-writer ? To read any—or all—of his half-dozen books is to find oneself indifferent to the answer. Best let that answer be—both. There was once a match at Colchester which Mr. Cardus attended on behalf of his newspaper, the *Manchester Guardian,* and he actually begins by describing the journey across Essex ! " The team went through fields stained with the crimson of poppies—fields that spread right and left to an horizon of trees. The team flashed by quiet country villages that have likeable names—Hatfield Peverel !—and now a glimpse would come of a windmill against the sky, and now a glimpse of a white house on a hill-top, or a cottage hiding under trees. . . ." And lest the reader who is impatient to get to the statistics and matter-of-fact details should be irritated by his unconventional way of describing a game, he reminds you that these things—journey, environment, weather—all matter a good deal if you would have a sense of the county a cricket team is standing for :

" In the match between Lancashire and Essex the willows round the field, the white tents, the river with curved wooden bridges over it near the pavilion, the country folk in the crowd—all these things had to do with the game. For cricket is sensitive to its habitation. Lancashire seemed a less workaday lot at Colchester than usually they seem ; years and years fell from their shoulders, and really there might have been a conspiracy going on at Colchester to change everybody into boys again. Lunch in a cool marquee was in itself enough to turn one back to schooldays ; and there was veal-and-ham pie, with ginger-beer to wash it down, and an old lady with a kindly face asking you with a curtsey if you wanted any more."

A technical knowledge of what you are writing about has never by itself equipped a writer for literature, and Mr.

Cardus avoids as much as he can what Mr. Kipling called the "filthily technical." But the practitioners of the game will find in his descriptions all they desire to learn of the mechanics of a particular match—and, on the other hand, those who dread statistics will imbibe them without knowing it, so softly and subtly toned down they become as he handles them. One of the most human essays he has yet written—poignantly human, beautifully human—is that on Johnny Briggs. Nevertheless, Mr. Cardus includes in it a technical analysis which puts to shame the old dull type of report, and incidentally makes one wonder how cricket lovers in the past could tolerate it. That he has made the earlier cricket reporter an anachronism is the triumph of this lovable, wise, humorous master—this Elia of cricket. It is a triumph made unique through sheer joy of the game—a spiritual as well as physical joy:

" Spooner and Maclaren—has a county possessed two batsmen who could begin an innings with more than their appeal to the imagination? They were as the King and the Prince, or as the eagle and the flashing swallow. Spooner was one of the cricketers who, when I was very young, made me fall in love with the game; I think of his batting now, in middle age, with gratitude. The delight of it all went into my mind, I hope, to stay there, with all the delight that life has given me in various shapes, aspects, and essences. When the form has gone—for it is material and accidental, and therefore perishable—the spirit remains. And Spooner's cricket in spirit was kin with sweet music, and the wind that makes long grasses wave, and the singing of Elisabeth Schumann in Johann Strauss, and the poetry of Herrick. Why do we deny the art of a cricketer, and rank it lower than a vocalist's or a fiddler's? If anybody tells me that R. H. Spooner did not compel a pleasure as æsthetic as any compelled by the most celebrated Italian tenor that ever lived I will write him down a purist and an ass."

Mr. Cardus is a master of the vignette in cricket portraiture. "Sutcliffe played his best cricket: he pulled and hooked with a bat that seemed to be admiring its own flourishes in a looking-glass. The sun shone on Sutcliffe's shiny hair and gave to him the halo that suits him perfectly. At the end of each over he leaned negligently on his bat and surveyed the scene; we could have sworn that he was cross-gartered." ... Cardus is also a master of re-creation. How well, through him, we know Shastbury and its school over the river, and the old cricket coach, William! ... And how well we know the heart-ache that he feels, we who, like him, have seen our well-loved heroes pass one by one from the green fields: "When Victor Trumper died he was a young man and a cricketer. The death of a cricketer before age has fallen on him is sad: it is even against nature. Well may he look down on our fields from his chill hall of immortality, far removed from the jolly flesh and blood of this life, and cry out 'Another day in the sun and wind and I not there, I not there!'" In another essay he writes: "On June days, when the trees beyond the Nursery End at Lord's are moving gently in the light, and cricketers are on the field with hours of the game before them—on these gracious mornings it is hard to understand why 'W. G.' should not have been permitted to go on living on the ripe earth, playing the game he loved until he was tired of it."

Much other prose by the "moderns" has in it a suggestion of the authentic music of bat against ball, ball against bat. Famous cricketers themselves have made their contributions—W. G. Grace, C. B. Fry (already mentioned) Richard Daft, Albert Knight, P. F. Warner, W. J. Ford, A. A. Mailey, C. G. Macartney, A. E. R. Gilligan, D. R. Jardine, P. G. H. Fender, Jack Hobbs, "Patsy" Hendren,

CRICKET IN PROSE AND VERSE

Maurice Tate, and R. C. Robertson-Glasgow, who perceived that cricket had its lighter side and, in witty and sparkling essays and rhymes, refuses to let the rest of us forget it. A. W. Pullin ("Old Ebor") and W. A. Bettesworth have set down their chats with other, less articulate, players. Mr. J. A. H. Catton has written at least one masterly descriptive essay—" Clem Hill's Face " : " The end was very near, and Hill dragged himself to long-on. Hirst smiled, and Rhodes, with a broad grin, showed his excellent teeth. Even Noble, saturnine though he be, was capable of a Mephistophelian laugh, but the eyes of Hill were downcast. He had not even a stray glance for an Australian dog. The somewhat sallow skin was absolutely blanched ; as white as the snow from heaven, before the flakes are contaminated by earth. It was a blessing that Clem could not see himself. His face might have frightened him. The bloodless visage was fit model for the painter of 'Despair.' . . . But the suspense and the agony ended. Rhodes finished his great innings of 6 not out by the winning hit. The silence was broken by a salvo of cheers, and Hill dashed ahead for the Pavilion in order to escape the invading thousands. It seemed to me as if his natural serenity instantly returned, for his face seemed to say : ' They've won the last match, but we shall take the ashes to Australia.' And they did."

A study of " The Jam Sahib of Nawanagar " by Mr. A. G. Gardiner is no less memorable. Here is the first paragraph :

" The last ball has been bowled, the bats have been oiled and put away, and around Lord's the grandstands are deserted and forlorn. We have said farewell to cricket. We have said farewell, too, to cricket's king. The game will come again with the spring and the new grass and the burgeoning trees. But the king will come no more. For the Jam Sahib is forty, and, alas ! the Jam Sahib is fat. And the temple bells are calling him back to his princely duties amid the sunshine, and the palm trees, and the spicy garlic smells of Nawanagar. No more shall we see him tripping down the pavilion steps, his face wreathed in chubby smiles; no more shall we sit in the jolly sunshine through the livelong day and watch his incomparable art till the evening shadows fall athwart the greensward and send us home content. The well-graced actor leaves the stage and becomes only a memory in a world of happy memories. And so 'hats off' to the Jam Sahib—the prince of a little State, but the king of a great game."

Andrew Lang, Mr. H. G. Wells (whose father was a county cricketer), E. F. Fay ("The Bounder"), Dean Hole ("On the Trent Bridge Ground at Nottingham I saw all the great heroes play"), Mr. J. B. Priestley, Mr. Robert Lynd ("When Bradman came out of the pavilion with his bat, you could have guessed that he was a man of genius even if you had never heard of him"), notably in a volume entitled *The Sporting Life;* a cricket lover who is content to be known as "Country Vicar"; Mr. Dudley Carew (*England Over*), Alec Waugh (let's drop the Misters now), Ivor Brown, Bernard Darwin, the late Sidney Pardon, an editor of *Wisden's Cricketers' Almanack*, Frank Thorogood, cricket correspondent of the London *News-Chronicle*, and half a dozen other gifted correspondents of wide reputation—Howard Marshall, H. J. Henley, R. B. Vincent (who succeeded A. S. Croome on *The Times*), H. A. H. Carson, G. W. Egdell, William Pollock, author of *The Cream of Cricket*), E. W. Swanton, Ronald Symond, Ivan Sharpe, Robin Baily, C. L. R. James (*Manchester Guardian*), one of our best newspaper writers who attend the daily play, John Bapty ("Littlejohn" of the *Yorkshire Post*)—what other English game has such an imposing array of authors, journalists, historians, ready-writers,

CRICKET IN PROSE AND VERSE

call them what you will? . . . As for the definitive historian, Mr. H. S. Altham, author of the classic *History of Cricket*, is supreme.

. . . This chapter has become fragmentary. Let it end in fragments. Delicious fragments. The fragrance of the " meadow-game with the beautiful name " is in them. There is the letter in *Our Village*, a literal copy—" For mistur jem browne blaxmith by S. Mistur browne this is to Inform you that oure parish plays bramley men next monday is a week, i think we shall lose without yew. from your humbell servant to command, Mary Allen." There is also the letter—a genuine one this time—from Mary Turner, East Hoathley, Sussex, written in September 1739 to her son. " Last Munday youre Father was at Mr. Payns and plaid at Cricket and came home please anuf for he struck the best Ball in the Game and whishd he had not anny thing else to do he ould play at Cricket all his Life." And (in *Practical Hints on Cricket*) a writer named William Clarke solemnly begins : " In altering your field, the bowler may have only one more ball to deliver in the over. Someone will be sure to say ' Oh, never mind till next over.' I don't believe in that doctrine." . . . It is with perhaps the most perfect fragment of all—by Sir James Barrie—that we would conclude : " A rural cricket match in buttercup time, seen and heard through the trees ; it is surely the loveliest scene in England and the most disarming sound. From the ranks of the unseen dead, for ever passing along our country lanes on their eternal journey, the Englishmen fall out for a moment to look over the gate of the cricket field and smile."

CHAPTER FIFTEEN

The Australians in England

(*How Our Village Tried to Play Them*)

BY HUGH DE SÉLINCOURT

CHAPTER FIFTEEN

The Australians in England

(*How Our Village Tried to Play Them*)

BY HUGH DE SÉLINCOURT

NO one knows or will ever know now how the secret leaked out, and turned what was to be essentially an informal and friendly affair into an event of national, nay, world-wide importance. It was natural enough that the latest Australian team should wish to have a go at the village which had been audacious enough even to dream of beating Mr. Armstrong's victorious eleven; and the match had been arranged on the understanding that they would turn up in time to start at 2.30 exactly like any other team: tea 5.0, draw 6.45 or 7.15 if there was anything in it: then a glass of beer perhaps at the pub and a nice drive home to their quarters in the cool of the summer evening. They had heard much of our pretty village grounds, which are unknown in Australia, all grass being burnt up by the heat, and were anxious to have a game on one. "Oh yes, pass the word round certainly in surrounding villages, boys; but keep it to yourselves, you understand, all private like and incog."

The news appeared first as a rumour (the match was entered X on the Tillingfold card); then the rumour was described as a hoax, which was fiercely denied. The British Broadcasting Corporation mentioned the matter in neat English with a courteous smile, and the world pricked up its ears. The thing suddenly became a gigantic stunt. The national game played in its natural surroundings ; the village green is the home of cricket ; a noble gesture illustrative of all that is finest in democracy ; the snobbery of Test Matches ; the fatal respect of persons degraded the freedom which was the birthright of every Briton. . . . There was no slogan, political or social or religious, that was not tacked somehow on to this little game. And astute financiers saw there was money in it ; the suggestion was actually made that the game should be played by artificial light at Olympia. But the climax was reached when Mr. Hitler, who dictates to a neighbouring country, decided that here was the golden opportunity for his Nazis to learn about the great English game in its simplest yet grandest form : the running commentary, translated into German, was to be broadcast throughout the length and breadth of his Reich, to battalions of Nazis drawn up in ranks to listen. Pictures of the game, with elucidatory comments, were to be thrown on every screen ; an intensive course of cricket culture (to be known always under drastic penalties as Hitler-ball) was arranged to start from this one game, which, as I have said, was intended to be a friendly and informal affair. The Soviet, French, and Italian Governments, growing suspicious, sent secret agents to investigate. Many serious persons wrote to serious papers urging the necessity for an international conference at Geneva, to discuss all possible implications, before an encounter which might have such far-reaching consequences on world welfare should take place.

The effect of all this publicity upon the village team was both distressing and unpleasant. Tillingfold had, for one reason and another, experienced some difficulty in raising a side at all that season. This world hubbub made it clear, as the great day drew nearer, that the difficulty of raising a side for this important match would be wellnigh insuperable. Natural diffidence caused our fellows to shrink

THE AUSTRALIANS AND OUR VILLAGE

from makin' monkeys of themselves, as one man put it; another man declined to be treated like a bloody film star and be paid nothing for his pains.

In consequence it became increasingly difficult to raise a side; but Mr. Gauvinier, faced with the ignominy of turning out one or even two men short when the eyes of the Empire were upon him, and of asking Mr. Woodfull to oblige him with a couple of substitutes when the ears of the world were pricked to catch his voice, eventually succeeded in getting a fairly representative side together, even though he was seriously upset by receiving an urgent message marked Strictly Confidential, from Headquarters, giving him a hint, large as the imprint of an elephant's foot and even weightier, as to the extreme inadvisability of employing in his attack upon the Australian batsmen anything even remotely resembling Leg Theory or anything that might possibly be construed into Leg Theory. In fact, under the circumstances, considering the unfortunate state of Japanese trade rivalry, it might be wiser perhaps to have no man at all, except a mid-on well back, upon the leg side when the more important batsmen were at the wicket.

Thus an avalanche of extraneous matter descended upon the game and bid fair to wreck and bury it, as the snow thundering down the mountain-side may wreck and bury an Alpine village.

On Wednesday morning the ground looked peaceful and smiling in the sunshine, as it usually looks of a fine morning; a few toddlers staggered about on the pleasant stretch of mown grass, as they usually do, greatly daring, but not too far from their prams and their mothers. The square on which the wickets were to be pitched waited expectant, full of promise, full of that happy promise which only a cricket ground packed with stored memories of good games won and good games lost can

BAT AND BALL

ever give in all its richness of unforgettable incident. On Wednesday afternoon came the first sign of what was to happen. A motor-car with trailer attached drew up by the gate leading into the ground; its occupants got out, looked round, saw a farm-house near, called at the farm, and were seen to return, slowly drive car and trailer into the adjoining field, and come to a slow stop. First one by one, they came, then in twos, then in threes, and settled in the adjoining fields, as gipsies come from all over England to settle on the course at Epsom. By Friday the thing began to look serious, and the British Broadcasting Corporation kindly consented to make a statement in their news bulletin to the effect that the cricket match which was undoubtedly to be played between Tillingfold and the Australians was essentially a friendly and intimate affair; that listeners should be reminded that the accommodation on a village ground was strictly limited, unlike Old Trafford or Trent Bridge or The Oval, where thousands could watch the play in comparative comfort. And so on and so on. The announcement was, of course, beautifully worded and exquisitely spoken, but its effect, however well intentioned, was unfortunate; for the average listener thought, " Oh that's all right, then; nobody will be turning up, so there'll be plenty of room for us ! " And forthwith determined to make a day of it.

From every town within reach, moreover (and what town now is not within reach?), charabanc and coach proprietors prepared excursion parties (with lunch and tea included in the fare) to see the match. On Friday night the stream of traffic began to flow; early on Saturday morning it was in full spate; from north and west and east, converging upon Tillingfold; a vast concourse of vehicles. By midday there were evidences of such a traffic block as had hitherto been unknown in the short history of motoring. The authorities, with the help of

THE AUSTRALIANS AND OUR VILLAGE

the A.A. and the R.A.C., did what they could, but they were powerless: our village policeman was wonderful, but what could one man effect against this national obsession? Mr. Gauvinier began to have serious fears that those of his team who went to work at any distance might be unable to reach their homes in time to have dinner and change; and that those who lived a mile or so outside the village would be unable to reach the ground at all. He was all right himself, as he could walk by field-paths most of the way; to bicycle, as was his usual practice, was quite out of the question. But what would others do? Just as he was leaving the house the telephone bell rang. He was thankful that he had not disconnected it, as rage and despair at its persistent ringing for the last twenty-four hours had prompted him to do; for it was Mr. Woodfull speaking. He was speaking from Shoreham. He had arranged, not without difficulty, to start an hour before his scheduled time, but they were properly stuck at Shoreham. Dreadful. Yes. Have you heard? No. What, the Soviet? Yes. Stalin's mad Hitler's got the jump of him; when he's decreed days ago all good Russians must take to cricket. Sure? Oh yes, Foreign Office rang me up at 10.25. Oh, we'll make it. Sure thing. And are you there? There's to be an American broadcast. Short-length wave. Yes. Sort of return for Kansas Derby. We'll get; but may be a trifle late. Some game. Yes. So long.

Mr. Gauvinier started on his walk to the ground, cursing the foolish circumstances which caused him, an oldish man, to start the afternoon with a one-and-a-half-miles' walk carrying a cricket bag. It seemed, too, a great shame that Italy, France, and Spain should be left out, as they appeared to be. He'd had such a happy time in Florence, he was half French; he'd always wanted to visit Spain, the home of Don Quixote and Sancho Panza. But the sight of the country lane that he was obliged to cross and along which he usually bicycled quietly to the ground scattered these altruistic broodings. It was, for as far as he could see, a solid jam of motor vehicles of every description, from baby cars to the most enormous coaches on which he had ever (having missed the last Motor Show) set his astonished eyes.

"You goin' to play in the match? Coo! Er! I'm comin' in tow!" Gauvinier pretended not to hear; but it was no good. The cry was taken up like magic or wireless loud-speakered, and soon a seething struggling mob (squabbling too, for it was shouted in expostulation, "How'll you ever find your way back to your seat, and what'll you do then, miles away from anywhere?") was swarming in his company along the shaded pathway, known as Lovers' Lane. He overheard: "Some sort of souvenir to show the kids," and became aware how violent and infectious is mass emotion, for he began to feel, as he quickened his pace, that he had somehow ceased to be a person and become merely (trousers, shirt, coat, bag, and bag's contents) a compendium of possible souvenirs, likely to be dispersed at any moment. A label on his cricket bag did the mischief: "It's Govineer, the village captain!" came an excited shout. He broke into a run; they gave chase, yelling to him, as tasty a morsel to his greedy pursuers as ever hare to hounds. Had he not, with great presence of mind, dropped his bag to leave them scrambling and struggling for its contents, it is doubtful what would have happened to him: probably what happens to a Russian traveller when overtaken by hungry wolves on the snow-clad steppes. As it was he reached the ground whole in body but ruffled in spirit, or rather he reached the next field but one adjoining the ground.

Tum demum, then and not till then (so slow is even a moderately intelligent mind to grasp a situation outside its previous experience) the full extent of the catastrophe, which publicity had wrought upon what should have been a rather specially good little game, broke upon his consciousness. He was, in fact, almost as nonplussed as the Higher Military Command by the events of the Great War. Like them, he simply did not know what to do. He could only murmur to himself, as he threaded his difficult way through cars and campers and hundreds ever anxious to press somehow nearer to the field of play: " All I know is this isn't cricket! " Bagless, bootless, batless, padless, capless, he eventually arrived at what had been the ground, and now resembled some weirdly arranged sort of car park : and he, the stickler for punctuality, heard the monastery clock chime three above the babel.

" Barely room for a tennis court," he sadly thought. " No room at all for Tim Wall's run—if he should get here."

" This is an outrage, sir," a furious voice accosted him. " An absolute disgrace. Do you realise this is a great occasion ? Are these the best arrangements you folk are capable of making ? Have you no sense of responsibility, no glimmer of what is fitting ? "

" Yes. Yes. But I've no cricket boots," was all Gauvinier could say.

" Grossly selfish and personal ! No thought for the good name of the country ; no thought for her prestige in the eyes of other nations. You saunter on to the ground half an hour late. It's an infamy ! "

" Yes. Yes. But I've no cricket boots," Gauvinier sadly repeated.

" Something's got to be done about it : and pretty sharp, too ! "

" Oh, I agree ! " said Gauvinier. " But I have never played without cricket boots before ! "

BAT AND BALL

High words might have arisen between the village captain and the enraged Broadcasting official had not, most fortunately, their attention been distracted by the manœuvres of an aeroplane flying uncommonly low.

"Gosh! It's an autogiro. Look, there are two of them."

All looked up; and large numbers were bumped in the back as they gazed up by eager photographers rushing forward with their cameras. "Not on the wicket, please," the distraught Gauvinier supplicated at the top of his voice, still thinking only of his wretched little game. His pitiful cry was not heard; with dismay he watched first one, then the other, slowly and beautifully alight upon the wicket. The crowd surged nearer to see Mr. Woodfull emerge with his cricket bag from the first; Mr. Bradman from the second. The cameras clicked; millions next day read the caption: *This picture shows Mr. Woodfull arriving on the Tillingfold ground, eager for his encounter with the village.*

Mr. Gauvinier found himself shaking hands with Mr. Woodfull, and murmuring foolishly:

"Awfully sporting of you to have turned up. All this"—he waved a rueful hand—"I'm most dreadfully sorry about it. Such a pretty little ground; never very large; now it is rather close quarters, I'm afraid."

And Mr. Woodfull, as behoves a visiting captain, remained dauntlessly courteous and cheerful, and assured him that he was certain they'd have a really jolly little game in spite of everything. Gauvinier shook a doubtful head.

"There's room perhaps to toss," he said, extracting a half-crown from his trouser pocket. But even so simple and so pleasant a matter of routine as the toss was not permitted to take place without interference. On the instant two or three excited photographers leaped forward crying out: "Just one moment, *please*!" in the harsh tone of authority curbing exasperation with incompetence. "It's more usual for captains to toss in front of the pavilion in their cricket kits."

"There is no front to the pavilion now; and I have no kit now . . ." Gauvinier mourned.

"We may waive that. Now, left hand lightly placed in left trouser pocket. So. Half-crown placed on right thumb-nail. So. Thank you. Your head turned slightly more this way. Mr. Woodfull, please, if you would step two paces nearer. Thank you. Three-quarter face to the camera." "Perhaps both gentlemen would not mind removin' their trilbies," suggested another photographer. "What about Mr. Bradman comin' into the picture," a third suggested, which enraged a fourth, who had been arranging to make a special and exclusive snap of *Don Bradman watching the skippers toss.*

"Take us or leave us!" said Mr. Woodfull, unused to be thus hectored, bluntly to the photographers, and added kindly to Mr. Gauvinier: "You just toss, old man."

But Mr. Woodfull's attention was distracted at that moment by the return of the autogiros. The welfare of his men was near to his heart, as it should be to the heart of every sound captain.

"Pack up, you fellows," he shouted unceremoniously. "Out of the way. Make a larger space, there. They must have room to alight."

And he started to signal frantically to the planes, waving his hat in one hand and his handkerchief in the other.

Meanwhile Mr. Bradman had slipped off, like the boy he is, merrily shouldering his way through the crowd, in search of cokernut shies which he felt must be lurking in such precincts and for which he has a very great liking. He is accustomed to visit the fairs round Melbourne and Sydney in a small Ford van in which to take home his winnings, or if he should go with Mr. Kippax or Mr. McCabe, in a Leyland lorry. The proprietors of these and kindred forms of amusement were not the least thankful among Australian sportsmen when no untoward circumstance prevented the great Test team of 1934 from sailing for the shores of England.

Now, too, Mr. Gauvinier's arm was gripped by the same Broadcasting official, by this time almost completely distraught.

" Something's got to be done about it," he babbled. " Something's got to be done about it. We can't go on describing the rural scene for ever. Nobody could."

" I tried to toss," Gauvinier excused himself.

" Such shocking management is a disgrace to the country. Do you mean to tell me an English crowd is so unsporting as to ruin the very thing they have come miles and at great personal inconvenience to see ? "

" I've told you nothing," Gauvinier said. " You can see for yourself it looks uncommonly like it. No one man by himself would do it ; a mass of men together does."

However, by four-thirty the last of the village team had fought his painful way on to what was left of the ground, dishevelled certainly, but determined (fair play being fair play) not to be crowded out of his well-earned Saturday's game by any mob of gaping sightseers. This proper bulldog spirit took them to the ground and then deserted them. They stood about miserably, powerless to help Gauvinier clear a slightly larger space around the poor pitch. But Mr. Gauvinier, elated at having been at last allowed to toss and at having won it, raised his voice and appealed to the better nature of the crowd : and what man has ever made such an appeal to an English crowd in vain ? By the time the last Australian, who happened to be Mr. Wall himself, arrived (engine trouble had delayed the gallant hop from Shoreham) Mr. Gauvinier was able to take him

THE AUSTRALIANS AND OUR VILLAGE

by the arm and show him how, with a little care, he might still have room for the full length of his admirable run to the wicket. This caused Mr. Gauvinier the very greatest satisfaction. Tea 7, draw 9. That was four hours. They'd get their little game. True, the ground was a bit confined and the autogiros had not improved the pitch: but Good Lord! one mustn't be fussy, and after all it would be the same for both sides, and a really sporting gentleman had returned him his boots and cap. Thus when just after five the Australians took the field (Sam Bird squeezing between motors had badly soiled his newly washed white umpire's coat) and Mr. Ballard and Mr. McCleod reached the wickets to bat, he felt almost at peace within and happy at the prospect of quite a decent little game, after all.

The crowd too were in the best of spirits. They appreciated being at such close quarters with the famous Australians, and felt quite safe, their glass screens being Triplex and suitably insured.

Mr. Woodfull adapted his field to the new conditions, and placed his men in a masterly manner, and with his well-known consideration for others arranged that after each ball his men should move one on in the small circle (more resembling kiss-in-the-ring perhaps than cricket), so that as many of the spectators as possible might have the joy of close proximity to all the great Australian players in turn.

But a large black cloud had been gathering, and as Mr. Wall, who was to open the bowling, began to walk slowly away to count the steps of his run, a drop (and it was a large one) fell upon his head. This caused him such surprise that he lost count and came slowly back to the wicket, and began once more. This time he reached the first car which he was obliged to pass, and in it was now sitting a fair (and she was very fair) occupant. Mr. Wall stopped dead. The perfectly behaved English crowd turned their heads

BAT AND BALL

to one side or whispered, " Will it rain ? " looking upwards, and to a man thought only what would have been shouted aloud by the rude barrackers on the Hill down under. They waited in respectful silence, broken at length by a clap of thunder and a sudden downpour of rain. It was a deluge. What man in the mass had failed to stop, the weather had. Over every other trick of fate these lion-hearted fellows had prevailed: but with the weather even cricketers themselves, like Gods with stupidity, fight in vain.

No European incident occurred. Mr. Hitler and Mr. Stalin remained quite unperturbed; and wholly satisfied with the phoned apologies of the Foreign Office, each addressed their young men, without a moment's hesitation, upon the duties of Nazi and Communist citizenship respectively. The young men had heard this before many times, but drawn up in ranks, as they were, at any rate they were temporarily kept from that mischief which another would-be dictator, Mr. Satan, is always anxious to find for idle hands (even when attached to Nazi or Communist wrists) to do.

So in the end all turned out really for the best in what is probably (though weather, women, and what-not might conceivably be improved) the best of all possible worlds.

CHAPTER SIXTEEN
A Love Match
BY A. G. MACDONELL

CHAPTER SIXTEEN

A Love Match

BY A. G. MACDONELL

THE annual cricket match between Eldersley Towers and Limberfold Hall is a desperately serious affair, for the two great country-houses are deadly rivals. It was in March 1925 that Lord Sigg, the famous financier, bought the Hall, and it was in April of the same year that Sir Jerusha Dibble, the famous financier, bought the Towers, and the flames of rivalry sprang up at once. Sir Jerusha, mortified at finding that he had missed being the senior squire of the district by a paltry fortnight, redressed the balance somewhat by adding an Elizabethan wing to his fine old Georgian mansion and buying four Rolls-Royce cars. Lord Sigg countered smartly with a Gothic annex, somewhat in the style of the Scott Memorial in Edinburgh, to his Carolean house, and six Daimlers.

Sir Jerusha built a village hall for the village of Eldersley Porcorum. Lord Sigg presented a cricket pavilion with lecture-room, shower-bath, and skittle-alley to Limberfold St. Eustace. His Lordship gave a tenner to the local branch of the British Legion. Sir Jerusha made it guineas. And so it was in everything.

The rivalry was not confined to the two great men. It spread vertically in the good old feudal fashion.

The butlers, of course, never met (county butlers never do) except on the one day in each year of the cricket match, when they bowed in a dignified silence that would have marked them out as men of the *haute noblesse* in a Louis Quinze salon. The valets and footmen, however,

BAT AND BALL

were less concerned with their dignity, and they took part in many crisp bouts of repartee in the local pubs (for the two villages were only a mile apart), while the bootboys frankly attacked each other on sight. The chauffeurs added to the gaiety of the district by trying to crowd each other into ditches, and, whenever a rival was behind, by driving as slowly as possible in the middle of the road.

But the flame of enmity was maintained at its purest heat of intensity by the two head-gardeners, who spread the most hideous accusations against each other's professional integrity. Thus the sudden plague of convolvulus which appeared in the azalea garden of Eldersley Towers in 1928 was unhesitatingly ascribed to handfuls of convolvulus-seed alleged to have been thrown over the Eldersley wall at dead of night by Limberfold minions. And there was, of course, the very painful incident at the joint Flower Show of the two villages when the mammoth, prize-winning pumpkin from Limberfold turned out to be a specially built and cleverly painted balloon, inflated with a bicycle pump through a valve that was cunningly hidden in the artificial stalk. Indeed, a hideous scandal was only averted by the chance discovery, which of course cancelled out the fraudulent pumpkin, that the Eldersley display of home-raised, brand-new, species of orchids—labelled ostentatiously O. Eldersleyensis, O. Sir J. Dibbleii, O. Lady Dibble, and O. Jerusha—had been imported in a special refrigerator from the world-famous orchidaceum in Oshkosh, Nebraska.

As for the villages, they had detested each other with the passionate hatred of the peaceful countryside ever since, so far as can be authoritatively ascertained, about A.D. 920, and they simply continued to do so.

The cricket match only added to the tenseness of the situation. For the six months from July to December in each year the recently played match was the sole topic of conversation in the pubs, and the collection of outstanding bets one of the main activities. From January to July, the forthcoming match, and the laying of fresh wagers, occupied everyone.

  *   *   *   *   *

The match of 1935 was an unusually critical one, even in such a series of critical matches, and by about the first week of May the tension between the two great houses was acute. There were several reasons for this. For instance, the second valet at Limberfold was walking out with the eleventh housemaid of Eldersley, and the Eldersley valets took it as a personal affront. Then Lord Sigg was known to have sold International Buttons at the wrong moment, whereas Sir Jerusha was known to have held on and cleaned up very nicely, and then Sir Jerusha had written a civil little note to his lordship, condoling with him on his losses and offering to advise him in future transactions on the Stock-market. Lord Sigg, in a cold fury, at once ordered a few Bentleys, and asked Sir Jerusha if he was thinking of selling the Towers, as he was looking about for a cosy little place for one of his grand-aunts, who was an old lady and did not get about much. And then, on top of all that, what must those young fools Dick Dibble, heir to the Towers, and the Hon. Angela Sigg, heiress to the Hall, do but pull the Montague-and-Capulet stuff and get engaged to be married a fortnight before the great match.

They were a tough young brace of eggs, and they had no illusion about what their beloved but not very much respected parents would say about it. And the parents said it, in no uncertain terms. " No," they both said, very firmly and in a whole variety of different ways, and with a remarkable wealth of expletive even for gentlemen who had been connected with the Stock Exchange.

Lord Sigg, of course, soon gave in. He had been giving

BAT AND BALL

in to Angela now for so long—for twenty-two years in fact, for she was born in 1913—that it had become a habit. Indeed, by this time neither of them ever noticed whether he had given in or not, such a meaningless formality had it become. Sir Jerusha's task was easier. It was not with a lovely, dark-haired, green-eyed, graceful daughter that he had to be firm, but with a rather ordinary, pleasant-faced boob of a son, who refused to bother about earning a living. So Sir Jerusha was firm, very firm indeed, firm almost to the point of nastiness, and talked a good deal about altering his will.

Dick, whose mental equipment was not up to the task of combating his formidable sire, went off gloomily and reported progress to Angela. Fortunately, Angela had more than enough intelligence for two, and within an hour the young man was back in his father's presence with a new proposition.

" Will you give me enough money to get married on, Father," he said, " if I fix it so that we beat old Sigg in the cricket match ? "

Sir Jerusha started visibly.

" Nobble 'em, eh ? " he said, putting his finger on the spot unerringly.

" Sort of," replied Dick.

" Can't be done," said the knight.

" How do you know, Father ? "

Sir Jerusha's ruddy countenance went even ruddier, and he coughed self-consciously.

" Anyway, it can't be done," he said àt last, walking over to the window, and looking out at the seven under-gardeners who were at that moment weeding the approach to the southern, or lesser, heronry.

" Why, did you ever try it, Dad ? " enquired Dick.

" There was no proof," cried Sir Jerusha sharply, wheeling round.

"Well, listen to this," said Dick. "If Angela invites the Sigg team this year, and if she invites a crowd so bad that we can't help winning, what about it, eh?"

"What about it?" shouted Sir Jerusha. "I'll tell you what about it. If that girl will nobble her own father and do a thing like that, then, by crikey, she's the girl for me and you can marry her the day after we win. But will she do it?" he went on anxiously.

"She'll do it, Dad. It was her own suggestion."

"What a girl," said Sir Jerusha, sinking his voice to a reverent whisper. "What a peach of a girl."

There was a pause and then the veteran financier went on more briskly, "Well, I'd better ring up Sigg and get a bet on with the old crook. No harm in making a little money on the side, eh, my boy? Eh, my boy? What?"

And Sir Jerusha, beaming delightedly, smacked Dick on the back and almost danced his way to the telephone.

  * * * * *

Next day the Hon. Angela Sigg took out her sports Alvis and proceeded to Chelsea, Bloomsbury, Fleet Street, and Hampstead, in search of eleven really bad cricketers. Sir Jerusha, on the other hand, having concluded a satisfactory wager with Lord Sigg, took the precaution of strengthening his team by inviting Mr. John Pobblewick, the famous amateur, who had bowled for England against Australia at Lord's some years before, to play for Eldersley in the great match.

  * * * * *

The great day was windless, blue-skyed, and sunny—a perfect day for cricket. It was the turn of Eldersley to be the hosts, and the staff of the Towers had been busy for days before, pitching the luncheon-marquees, rolling out the beer and cider barrels, painting the boundary flags and the numbers for the score-board, and mowing and rolling the pitch.

Sir Jerusha was in high good humour. His team had all arrived the night before, and a cleaner-limbed, better-tubbed body of young men he had seldom had the pleasure of clapping eyes upon. After an abstemious dinner they had practised their catching on the lawn for half an hour and had all retired to bed at ten o'clock sharp. Very different had been the scene over at the Hall, according to information received by Sir Jerusha from his butler, who had got it from the eleventh housemaid, who had got it from her boy-friend, the second Limberfold valet. His lordship's team, it appeared, was very different from his former teams. This year it consisted of men with longish hair and red faces, men with loud voices and gusts of roof-shaking laughter, men who all talked simultaneously, and, above all, men with truly stupendous thirsts.

" Twenty-seven bottles of his lordship's best champagne," the butler reported with awe in his voice, " and they broke into the cellar and got the last fifteen themselves, because his lordship thought a dozen was enough, and one of them fell over a bin of '96 port and smashed the lot, sir, and they all sat down on the floor of the cellar and cried. And then it appears, sir, they found his lordship's old Napoleon brandy and they drank a couple of magnums of that and started laughing again."

" When did they go to bed, Parker ? " asked Sir Jerusha, chuckling and rubbing his podgy hands together.

" I am informed, sir, that four of them were carried upstairs at 3.30 a.m., that three others retired at 5 a.m., and that the remaining four were found this morning by the gardeners, sir, climbing in his lordship's new rock-garden. They were in full evening dress and were roped together, sir, being under the impression that they were climbing the Matterhorn. I understand, sir, that the frequent ice-steps, as it were, which they thought it necessary to dig, or cut, as you might say, sir, have not materially improved his lordship's rock-garden."

"Good lads, good lads," exclaimed Sir Jerusha, and then he added, greatly to the butler's mystification, "What a girl, what a peach of a girl."

The butler coughed discreetly. "I may say, sir," he said, "that, news of these events having spread in the neighbourhood, the betting is now eighteen to one on us, sir."

"And I've got an even ten thousand with the old fool," roared Sir Jerusha in an ecstasy of glee. "Serve champagne at luncheon, Parker, and plenty of it. None of your miserly dozen. We'll fix 'em."

Dick smiled a quiet smile when he heard the news. Brains and beauty! What a marvellous girl.

Punctually at eleven o'clock the house team was waiting outside the pavilion, resplendent in beautifully creased flannels, blazers, scarves, and caps. Mr. Pobblewick was wearing his England cap. The deck-chairs on the edge of the ground near the pavilion were rapidly filling up with elegant frocks, parasols, and silk stockings, while on the other side two large separate groups of spectators, lying on the grass or sitting on long benches, showed that the village partisans were in strong force. Everything, in fact, was ready except the visiting team. At 11.15 the Eldersley team began to bowl to each other in a desultory sort of way, but by 11.30 they were beginning to look at wrist-watches and to scan the horizon. Finally, at 11.40, Lord Sigg, with a face of thunder, arrived in a huge motor with four of his daughter's eleven.

They were Sir William Biffington, the famous poet, Messrs. Belton and Drury, dramatic critics, and Mr. Whistle, an actor. Sir William was wearing an ancient pair of linen trousers, Mr. Belton's pair were grey with a thin white stripe, and Mr. Drury took off his coat and revealed an elegant blue and yellow football shirt which fastened at the throat with a string arrangement. Mr. Whistle was immaculate but rather drunk, and he gazed round with a sort of owlish benevolence and invariably addressed the livid Lord Sigg as " laddie."

The Eldersley team were aghast. Never before had they seen such fearful clothes. Pobblewick took Dick aside and whispered, " Make them bat first if you win the toss. Let's get it over quickly." Dick nodded. He would have agreed to anything that morning. The match was as good as won and Angela was as good as his.

There was, however, a considerable delay before the coin could be spun, for first of all the visiting quartette caught a glimpse of a champagne bottle in one of the marquees, and they disappeared with miraculous rapidity. Then, after they had been run to earth, they all claimed the captaincy of the team and a warm wrangle was soon in full swing, and then the wrangle resolved itself into an academic discussion about the priority of the Arts. Sir William and Mr. Whistle agreed that criticism was not an Art at all, but disagreed between poetry and drama ; the two critics held together for their profession, but quarrelled about their respective newspapers. Then Mr. Belton suggested that Dick should toss against his own vice-captain, but Sir William pointed out rather shrewdly that that would materially reduce the Limberfold chance of winning the toss, and the deadlock was only settled by the arrival of a fifth member of the Limberfold team, Mr. Twigg, a distinguished novelist. Mr. Twigg was in full evening dress, complete with silk hat, and the other four, dazzled by his appearance, instantly elected him captain. The coin was spun. Mr. Twigg called wrongly, and Dick asked him to bat first.

" Certainly," said Mr. Twigg, turning to his men. " Two of you bat, a third hold himself in readiness, a

A LOVE MATCH

fourth to go out to umpire, while I will endeavour to find more suitable apparel. I appear to have mistaken the nature of this jamboree." He looked down at his costume with an air of surprise. "My attire seems only suitable," he added, "for dining, waiting at table, or being married in France.

"The essence of our position," continued Mr. Twigg to his team, after they had got back into the champagne tent, "is to hold the fort until such time as reinforcements arrive. I take it that reinforcements will arrive, by the way?"

"Sammy and young Pie-face are up," said Sir William, "I saw them throwing billiard-balls at the swans on the lake as we came along. Old Sigg was crazy about it!"

"Why? They weren't hitting them, were they?" asked Mr. Whistle in surprise.

"Oh, no," replied Sir William.

"Well, we must do the best we can," said Mr. Twigg. "Out you go and try to hold the fort till lunch."

Ten minutes later, that is to say sharp at 12.25, the great match began.

Sir William prepared to receive the first ball, Mr. Pobblewick of Cambridge, Surrey, and England, to bowl it, and the first of the many strange incidents which made this match so extraordinary took place at once. The first ball was loudly "no-balled" by the umpire. Mr. Pobblewick was surprised.

"Was I over the crease or outside it?" he asked mildly.

"Neither," said the umpire, who was none other than Mr. Whistle, the actor. "You were throwing."

"What!" cried the outraged Test-match player.

"You were throwing," replied Mr. Whistle, with dignity.

Mr. Pobblewick, white with rage, bowled again and was

no-balled again. This time he said nothing, but handed the ball to his captain, and walked off the field. Dick Dibble ran after him and tried to soothe the outraged warrior, but all his blandishments were in vain and he was forced to return and depute his first-change bowler to take up the attack. The new bowler, a medium-paced left-hander who had played for Northamptonshire, took a little time in rearranging his field, and Sir William took a little more in taking new guard, and then Mr. Whistle intervened again with the blandest possible smile.

"I'm sorry," he said, addressing Dick, "but I am afraid you can't do this. The bowler who began the over must finish it."

"He's not going to play any more," explained Dick.

"He must finish the over," replied the adamantine umpire, and so Dick had to go off and persuade Mr. Pobblewick, who had already half-changed out of his flannels, to come back so that the game might continue.

It was 12.45 before the third ball of the match was delivered by a very sulky England bowler, and it was a very slow underhand full-pitch to leg which Sir William hit out of the ground with his well-known flail-stroke.

The remaining five balls of the over were identical and were dispatched into the same field by the delighted knight. Mr. Pobblewick, his duty done, then retired from the field for good, accompanied by the good-natured, jovial cat-calls of the Limberfold villagers, and the savage boos and hisses of the Eldersleyites who were appalled to see 38 runs being scored against them in the very first over of the match. Their spirits rose, however, when Mr. Belton was dismissed by the third ball of the second over, and when Mr. Drury fell backwards over his wicket in attempting to play the fourth ball. After a short pause Mr. Twigg himself came in, having borrowed some flannels and a shirt, but still wearing his suède-topped, pearl-buttoned boots,

A LOVE MATCH

and there was a long delay while he insisted on having the sightscreen moved, backwards and forwards, an inch or two at a time. He succeeded in stopping the last two balls of the over and, as it was now one o'clock, luncheon was announced. The fort had been held, and the six stragglers of the Limberfold team, consisting of two journalists, a painter, a playwright, another poet, and another novelist, arrived at that precise moment in an ancient wagonette drawn by a cart-horse and a small patient donkey, and they were singing an old French marching-song at the tops of their not inconsiderable voices.

Luncheon was a painful affair. One team sat in dead silence at one end of the long trestle-table, the other roared and sang at the other. And amid the noise could be heard sometimes the silvery laughter of Angela.

After luncheon was over, Lord Sigg made his last appeal to his by now hilarious eleven. He took them aside and began, almost with tears in his eyes, "I know it isn't any use with literary gentlemen like you offering you money——"

"What!" exclaimed the eleven literary gentlemen simultaneously.

Lord Sigg wrung his hands. "I knew it would be an insult," he moaned.

"Insult, my eye," exclaimed Sir William, who, being a poet, had a very competent grasp of worldly affairs. "How much?"

Lord Sigg was bewildered. "Do you mean to say that you would accept a present of twenty-five pounds apiece if you win this match?"

"We do," was the emphatic and simultaneous reply. "The only question is 'how,'" added Sir William thoughtfully, and, "Why the devil didn't you tell us before?" said Mr. Twigg with some petulance. "We could have collected Larwood and Voce or someone."

"My daughter said you were all county players and that you were certain to win," bleated Lord Sigg.

"Look here," said Sir William Biffington abruptly; "have your villagers and retainers and what-nots been betting on us?"

"Heavily," said his lordship, "and so have I," he added plaintively.

"Very well," replied the poet. "I declare our innings closed."

"Hey!" cried Mr. Twigg. "You're not the captain. I am."

"If we're to get this money," answered Sir William gravely, "you must do as I tell you."

The remainder of the team, with a sad fickleness, instantly voted for the deposition of Mr. Twigg and the election of Sir William, while Lord Sigg sat down on a bench and buried his face in his hands.

The news spread like wild-fire. Limberfold had declared at 38 for two wickets after two overs. Things began to happen at once. Firstly, three of the star Eldersley batsmen announced that they had never been so damnably treated in their lives, and that if anyone thought they were going to waste a Saturday afternoon clowning about with a lot of mountebanks, they were jolly well mistaken, and they collected their cricket-bags, got into their motor-cars, and drove away. Dick made little effort to detain them. He wanted to get the match over as soon as possible, and he still had seven (for Pobblewick had also departed) perfectly good cricketers to score 39 runs on a plumb wicket.

The second result of the premature declaration was, as the crafty Sir William, poet, and therefore expert in psychology, had anticipated, a wild burst of fury among the Limberfold supporters, who jumped to the conclusion that the whole thing was a put-up job on the part of their hated rivals to cheat them on their wagers. It required, therefore, but little encouragement from Sir William, acting as *agent provocateur* in a disguise of a raincoat and a bowler belonging to one of the butlers which he had found hanging in the pavilion, to invade the ground and start kicking their heels into the wicket. The sight of this was too much for the lads of Eldersley and they rushed to the rescue, and in a moment there was a very pretty free-for-all in full swing on the pitch. While it was in progress, and all eyes were fixed on the fight or being blacked in it, Sir William might have been seen talking earnestly to Mr. Jaggin, the Limberfold policeman, and a close observer might even have seen a piece or two of paper passing surreptitiously from the knightly to the constabulary hand. However that may be, it is certain that a few minutes later P.C. Jaggin accosted one of the Eldersley players, a minor-counties batsman of some distinction, and requested him to accompany him to Limberfold police-station to give an account of his movements on the morning of the 27th ult. Protesting vehemently, but nevertheless bowing, in true British fashion, to the Majesty of the Law, the player departed with Mr. Jaggin, and Dick suddenly found that he had only six players, of whom two were bowlers pure and simple, with which to make 39 runs on a wicket that now looked, after the fracas had been quelled and the combatants persuaded to retire across the boundary, as if a whippet tank had been dragging a harrow backwards and forwards over it. He hastened up to Mr. Twigg.

"I say, sir, we must change the pitch," he said. Mr. Twigg shook his head. "I am no longer captain of our eleven," he observed mournfully. "Bill Biffington is captain now."

Somewhat surprised at this novel change of leadership, Dick went in search of the poet, and at last found him sitting under an elm tree writing a ballade on the lining which he had torn out of a Free Forester straw-hat that someone had carelessly left lying on a deck-chair.

Dick made his proposal, but Sir William was immovable. "I would do it if I could," he kept on saying, " but it's against the rules, and we must keep to the rules."

"But the pitch is in a terrible state," cried Dick in consternation. "If you've got a fast bowler, it will be simple murder."

"I myself am a bowler of exceptional speed," replied the knight modestly, and he added another line to his poem.

"Well, I suppose I must do the best I can with the heavy roller," said Dick gloomily. He was not quite so happy about the outcome of the match now. Sir William sprang to his feet and hauled an enormous watch out of his trouser pocket.

"Sorry," he said, " I'm afraid there isn't time for that. Already more than the statutory forty minutes for luncheon have elapsed. We must start as soon as the umpire calls 'Play.' The side refusing to play within two minutes loses the match. Rule Forty-five." He made a cup of his hands and roared, "Whistle, out you go and umpire and call 'Play' at once."

Dick sprinted to the pavilion and got into pads and gloves in time to reach the wicket with a colleague before the two minutes had elapsed after Mr. Whistle had called "Play."

Sir William was the bowler. Now Sir William had never bowled in his life, but one glance at the torn and scarred wicket showed him that this was no occasion for orthodox methods. It was a case, as in warfare, for what the experts call the Weapon of Surprise, and he ambled up to the wicket and bounced the ball in the neighbourhood of his feet. The ball, when it started off on its long journey towards the other wicket, was going comparatively straight. On its fourth and fifth bounces, however, it turned sharply to leg and was ultimately retrieved by the square-leg umpire. The second ball, conversely, started towards point and gradually worked its way inwards over the furrows and pits until Dick felt that he ought to pay some attention to it. He blocked it, therefore, with his bat, picked it up, and politely returned it to Sir William.

" How's that? " roared the entire fielding side. Mr. Whistle's finger pointed inexorably to the heavens, and the Eldersley mob sprang into action once again in a frantic burst of rage. But before the jubilant Limberfoldians had time to mobilise in defence, Mr. Whistle had stalked across the field and announced to the Eldersleyites in tones that Henry Irving might have envied, " Out for handling the ball, without being requested to by the opposite side. Rule twenty-nine."

The next batsman was a wary player, and he watched the erratic approach of the ball with a hawk-like eye, and struck it beautifully past cover for an easy single. But most unfortunately as he was running towards the other wicket he somehow, quite inexplicably, bumped into Sir William, who fell heavily to the ground.

" How's that? " roared the fielding side, and again Mr. Whistle's finger pointed heavenward, and he shook his head sadly. " Rule thirty," he said dreamily, " Obstructing the field."

The silence that settled down like thunder over the Eldersley partisans was more eloquent of approaching storms than any vocal demonstrations could have been. Limberfold, on the other hand, were wildly jubilant.

Sir William's next ball was a strange one. Elated by his success at capturing two cheap wickets, he attempted to bowl a much faster one and, employing a sort of slinging, round-arm action, he hurled the ball violently at the opposing batsman. Unfortunately he let go of it a little too soon and it soared high over the wicket, and landed on the fourth waistcoat button of an elderly J.P. who was taking a comfortable nap in a deck-chair on the boundary. Mr. Whistle reluctantly had to perform the unique ceremony of signalling six wides.

Sir William was undaunted, and slung down another tremendous ball. This time, however, he held on much too long and the ball struck the ground almost at once. But it did not bounce. It must have hit some very odd contour, for it shot straight forward at a high rate of speed along the ground, and then, just as it reached the batsman, it must have hit another very odd contour, for it reared straight up into the air and connected precisely upon the point of the batsman's nose. Whimpering in agony, the unfortunate man retired to the pavilion and refused to take any further part in the game.

But his agony was as nothing compared with the agony of Dick and Angela. Talking in frenzied whispers behind the score-tent, they discussed the calamitous situation. " We've only got two more men," muttered Dick hoarsely, " and Hobbs himself wouldn't make thirty on that pitch against those fiends and their damned umpire. Dad will lose ten thousand quid and I'll be cut off with a farthing. Oh, Angela, what are we to do ? " He almost wrung his hands, but, being a British public-school boy, he just managed to refrain from this hideous solecism.

Angela tapped her shoe thoughtfully with her parasol and gazed at the sky. Dick gazed at Sir Jerusha, who was striding up and down with his hands behind his back and his face purple.

" Dad's bribed them, of course," she remarked, still gazing at the sky.

" But poets don't care about money," expostulated Dick.

" Oh yeah ? " replied Angela inelegantly.

A great roar from the Eldersley partisans interrupted them. They turned and saw the ball being thrown back

A LOVE MATCH

from the boundary. The next moment there was a Limberfold roar as the next ball broke sharply from the off, thence twice in succession from the leg, and then once again from the off, and shot against the foot of the middle stump.

Dick groaned. " Only one more man, and twenty-eight still to get. We're done."

" Listen," said Angela urgently. " Our only chance now is to get a draw out of it. That's better than losing outright. Look at that storm coming up," and she pointed with her parasol to a mass of black clouds that was advancing rapidly. " If we can only delay the game for a quarter of an hour, we will be saved yet."

" But how ? " asked Dick helplessly.

" By taking champagne out to the fielding side, of course," said Angela.

" Darling, you're a genius," he cried, and raced off to the refreshment tent.

The fielding side were enchanted with such hospitality. It was barely three o'clock, and here was the Roederer coming out again.

Forgetting all about the game, they clustered round the trays and fell to with zest. Nor did they pay the slightest attention to the furious exhortations of the weather-wise Limberfoldians to " get on with the game." Those old farmers knew what that storm-cloud meant.

Sir Jerusha, into whose ear Angela had been melodiously whispering, looked up at the sky, and his face brightened. " If I don't win, at least I won't lose," he muttered.

" And do I get Dick if it's a drawn match ? " enquired Angela.

" I didn't say so," said Sir Jerusha cautiously.

" If I don't," said Angela casually, " I'll tell the world how you bribed me to fake the match."

Sir Jerusha started violently. "Blackmail, eh, you hussy?"

Angela nodded and smiled a sweet smile.

"Well, damme, if you aren't a peach of a girl," exclaimed the former finance-pirate in admiration. "All right. You shall have him."

At that moment there was a flash of lightning, a clap of thunder, and the rain came down in sheets.

* * * * *

So ended one of the most remarkable cricket matches in history. Play lasted from 12.25 until 3.40, and in spite of that only three overs were bowled, and in spite of that again the match was within an ace of being brought to a definite conclusion.

The two teams dined together at Eldersley Hall, and Dick and Angela announced their engagement. After tumultuous cheering, Sir William Biffington proposed their health in an impromptu speech that was so full of poetry and grace that it moved even Lord Sigg to tears. "Dammit," he said to the poet after he had sat down, "you didn't win my match for me, but you shall get your twenty-five pounds all the same."

"What twenty-five pounds?" said Sir William. "Pass the champagne."

CHAPTER SEVENTEEN

From the Pavilion

BY THOMAS MOULT

CHAPTER SEVENTEEN

From the Pavilion

BY THOMAS MOULT

> . . . Always the same
> Old talk with laughter rounding off each tale—
> Laughter of friends across a pint of ale
> In the blue shade of the pavilion.

A CATCH came to A. C. Maclaren out in the deep field during a game in Australia. Somebody at the ringside shouted as the ball lingered in the air:
" Miss it, Archie, and you can kiss my sister ! "
To Maclaren's eternal credit he took the catch and missed the sister.

Jack Hobbs tells this story in *Playing for England*. It is the best ever told about A. C. Maclaren. Here is the best about Hobbs (if it is about Hobbs)—told by himself:

" It was during this tour (1909–10 in South Africa) that Wilfred Rhodes and I began our many first-wicket partnerships and embarked on our famous short-run business. We astonished the natives in this: they could not believe that we had no secret signals.

" There was once a pair of batsmen who tried to make their signals very secret indeed. Their plan was: 'When I say No, you run; when I say Yes, don't.' And they always succeeded in running themselves out.

" ' Wilf ' and I took care not to follow their example." . . .

From Hobbs to Grace. When W. G. was touring Canada and America in 1872, his hosts at the various functions called upon him to make an after-dinner speech.

BAT AND BALL

Here it is, as originally delivered at Montreal, and also with the variations made at the other places :

"Gentlemen, I beg to thank you for the honour you have done me. I never saw better bowling than I have seen to-day, and I hope to see as good wherever I go."

The Ottawa speech followed a few days later : " Gentlemen, I beg to thank you for the honour you have done me. I never saw a better ground than I have seen to-day, and I hope to see as good wherever I go."

Then at Toronto : " Gentlemen, I beg to thank you for the honour you have done me. I never saw better batting than I saw to-day, and I hope to see as good wherever I go."

Also at Toronto : " Gentlemen, I beg to thank you for the honour you have done me. I never met better fellows than I have met to-day, and I hope I shall meet as good wherever I go."

At Hamilton he said : " Gentlemen, I beg to thank you for the honour you have done me. I have never seen prettier ladies than I have seen to-day, and I hope I shall see as pretty wherever I go."

Finally, at New York : " Gentlemen, I beg to thank you for the honour you have done me. I have never tasted better oysters than I have tasted here to-day, and I hope I shall get as good wherever I go." . . .

So many " best " stories are circulated about the Grand Old Man of cricket that another is admissible here. W. G. had numerous arguments with the umpire, and he invariably came off triumphant. In one match, when bowling, he appealed for l.b.w. against the batsman.

" Not out," said the umpire.

Grace asked again a few overs later, and on receiving the same reply muttered as he passed the umpire : " I'll have him yet." Every over after that he hit the batsman on the leg, but instead of appealing he kept on muttering—always

FROM THE PAVILION

so that the umpire could hear: "I'll have him yet, I'll have him yet."

At last the worthy Doctor struck the batsman such a crack on the leg and whipped round triumphantly to the umpire with: "What did I tell you?"

"Out," said the umpire. . . .

Cecil Parkin, the old English and Lancashire bowler, has told one of the best umpire stories. It was the day of a local "Derby," and before the match the president of the visiting eleven went on the field to look at the wicket. When he got into the "middle," an old man was there, with white whiskers and a stick.

The president got into conversation with this oldest of old inhabitants. "Well," he said, "it's a good wicket, and we'll have a keen game."

"Ay, ay, sir," replied Methuselah, "we 'ave a reight good side this year."

"Let's see," said the president, "who is getting most of your wickets this season?"

"Why, sir," replied the old man, "I be getting the most."

"Good heavens!" cried the president. "You don't mean to say that you can bowl at your time of life?"

"No, sir," replied Methuselah, "I ain't no bowler—I'm the umpire!" . . .

Mr. H. D. G. Leveson-Gower, one of the present-day leaders of cricket politics, recalls an umpire who was very interested in a club match on a famous London ground. Only a few runs were wanted for victory; the bowler sent down a ball well off the leg stump. The ball hit the batsman's leg and an appeal followed.

"Out!" shouted the umpire immediately, and, whipping off the bails, exclaimed: "*We've* won!" . . .

A "best" story about a batsman:

He played in a league match and stood too much on

ceremony when he reached the wicket. He took his guard with all the care and " swank " of a county cricketer ; then he had the sightscreen moved ; then he changed guard and marked out his new guard with the bail ; then he looked round the field, hitched up his trousers, adjusted his cap, and took the first ball.

It clean bowled him, and as he was passing cover-point on his way back to the pavilion, the fieldsman, being a humorist, said :

" 'Ard luck, sir. Just as you were getting set ! " . . .

The next story concerns a fieldsman. Incidentally he was " Patsy " Hendren, and it is the best about that great little favourite whose home is Lord's.

" I was out in the Bush in Australia watching a match, when I was asked to play. I was, of course, quite unknown to the other players. I consented. My side lost the toss and I was promptly sent to field at deep square-leg, where I found myself at the bottom of a hill, not doing a thing, and the match going on !

" I kept throwing the ball back whence it came, and they kept me there all day. At length I had one hit to me that did not touch the edge of the cliff (as it might be called)—a catch. Carrying the ball in my hand, I made for the wicket. It was quite a few seconds before I reached the summit of the hill, and when I did I shouted : ' I've caught it ! I've caught it ! '

" They all glared at me, and after a time informed me that I had caught one of my own side out ! "

Hendren told the story himself to William Pollock (" Googly "), who prints it in his book, *The Cream of Cricket*, where there are many other stories and storyettes as good. . .

The best story ever told by S. M. J. Woods :

" On one occasion C. I. Thornton, A. J. Webbe, George Vernon, and Percy de Paravicini came to breakfast with us on the second day of the match *v.* C. I. Thornton's England XI. There were seven hot lobsters for breakfast, bacon and eggs, and cold tongue. When the captain saw the lobsters, he remarked : ' Good Lord, we can't eat hot lobsters for breakfast ! ' I remarked : ' Well, I'm sorry, but if you can't you will have to do without fish this morning.' I think one of them tried it and ate well. Mac (Gregor MacGregor) and I didn't have bacon and eggs, or cold tongue, as they were lovely birds, those lobsters, washed down with Jesus audit ale. The game was continued, and I took all ten wickets against them, and we won by four wickets." . . .

Story of a hitter :

He had lifted the ball twice over the fence for six—without lifting his feet. A third time he did so, and this time he *did* lift his feet. Then the wicket-keeper heard him mutter, as he watched the ball soaring away into the horizon :

" Cripes, if only I'd got hold of that one ! " . . .

Story of a stonewaller :

> Block, block, block,
>   At the foot of thy wicket, O Scotton !
> And I would that my tongue could utter
>   My boredom. You *won't* put the pot on !
> O, nice for the bowler, my boy,
>   That each ball like a barndoor you play !
> O, nice for yourself, I suppose,
>   That you stick at the wickets all day !
>
> And the clock's slow **hands** go on,
>   And you still keep up your sticks ;
> But O for the lift of a smiting hand,
>   And the sound of a swipe for six !
> Block, block, block,
>   At the foot of thy wickets, ah, do !
> But one hour of Grace or Walter Read
>   Were worth a week of you !

Punch printed it, long, long ago. . . . M. A. Noble's best story—a true one—is also about a stonewaller, in Australia. A Sydney crowd became very impatient at the slow scoring. One man yelled out : " Put Bettington on." Soon afterwards he yelled again, this time : " Put Bradman on ! " He was answered by a voice from another quarter of the ground : " Put the clock on ! " . . .

Now for a story, also by " Monty " Noble, about A. P. F. Chapman, captain of England during the tour in Australia of 1928-9, and Philip Mead, a member of his team. At the civic reception in Brisbane the Lord Mayor referred sincerely to the pleasure it gave Australians to greet again the heroes of former tours, mentioning Chapman, Hobbs, Tate, Sutcliffe, Hendren, and Freeman. During his reply, Chapman tactfully and subtly remedied an omission. " You appear to have overlooked one of the members of the side, my Lord Mayor," he said, " in the shape—no, pardon me, in the *form* of Phil Mead." When the laughter had subsided Chapman went on to recount that in Sydney during that tour an enthusiast had sought out Mead, shaken him by the hand, and remarked, " I knew your father when he was out here in 1911." . . .

. . . Of Victor Trumper. By Jack Hobbs. " Trumper was a big personality as well as a cricketing genius. Everybody felt his charm, and even the Sydney schoolboys knew of his generosity, for he had a sports outfitter's business, and somebody told me that if a youthful customer found the price of a bat too much for him, why, ' Vic ' hadn't the heart to let him go out of the shop without it ! This explains, perhaps, why Trumper never made a fortune out of business." . . .

Another story from *Punch*. In a cartoon so long since as August 1863, when John Jackson, the fast bowler, was in his prime. The Pride of the Village, with his left arm in a sling and his left knee bandaged, is saying :

FROM THE PAVILION

" I 'ad a hover of Jackson : the first ball 'it me on the 'and ; the second 'ad me on the knee ; the third was in my eye ; and the fourth bowled me out ! Jolly game."

This reminds me, wrote Mr. J. A. H. Catton in *Wickets and Goals*, of the story that Alec Watson used to tell of the match between A. N. Hornby's team and the Lancashire Constabulary. A ball from John Crosland struck a policeman on the foot. He flung his bat down and hopped about in pain. At length he picked up his bat and began walking towards the pavilion.

"Here, you're not out," said Watson. "I know," answered the policeman, " but I'm goin'."

Finally, here is the best story ever told about P. F. Warner.

. . . And a broken umbrella. In a ringside seat at Lord's was a spectator who abused loudly and somewhat offensively the Middlesex team in general, and one of their number in particular. In the end the particular victim happened to be fielding close to the spectator, whose umbrella chanced to be leaning on the ropes. In trying to save a four the fielder found himself unable to avoid the umbrella, and broke it.

At the close of play the man, bursting with indignation, demanded retribution. It was a ticklish case. " Plum " Warner was sent to deal with him. He summarily dissolved all the man's arguments by demanding to know by what right his umbrella had been on the field of play !

CHAPTER EIGHTEEN

" Ancient and Modern "

(The First Code of Rules and the Latest)

CHAPTER EIGHTEEN

" Ancient and Modern "

(*The First Code of Rules and the Latest*)

I

ANCIENT—1744

YE pitching of ye first Wicket is to be determined by ye cast of a piece of Money.

When ye first Wicket is pitched and ye popping Crease cut, which must be exactly 3 Foot 10 Inches from ye Wicket ye other Wicket is to be pitched, directly opposite, at 22 Yards distance, and ye other popping Crease cut 3 Foot 10 Inches before it.

Ye bowling Creases must be cut, in a direct line, from each Stump.

Ye Stumps must be 22 Inches, and ye Bail 6 inches.

Ye Ball must weigh between 5 and 6 Ounces.

When ye Wickets are both pitched and all ye Creases cut, ye Party that wins the toss up may order which Side shall go in first at his option.

Laws for Ye Bowlers 4 Balls an Over

Ye Bowlers must deliver ye Ball with one foot behind ye Crease even with ye Wicket, and when he has bowled one ball or more shall bowl to ye number 4 before he changes Wickets, and he shall change but once in ye same Innings.

He may order ye Player that is in at his Wicket to stand on which side of it he pleases at a reasonable distance.

If he delivers ye Ball with his hinder foot over ye bowling

BAT AND BALL

Crease, ye Umpire shall call No Ball, though she be struck, or ye Player is bowled out, which he shall do without being asked, and no Person shall have any right to ask him.

Laws for Ye Strikers, or those that are in

If ye Wicket is Bowled down, its Out.

If he strikes, or treads down, or falls himself upon ye Wicket in striking, but not in over running, its Out.

A stroke or nip over or under his Batt, or upon his hands, but not arms, if ye Ball be held before she touches ye ground, though she be hug'd to the body, its Out.

If in striking both his feet are over ye popping Crease and his Wicket put down, except his Batt is down within, its Out.

If he runs out of his Ground to hinder a catch, its Out.

If a ball is nipped up and he strikes her again, wilfully, before she comes to ye Wicket, its Out.

If ye Players have cross'd each other, he that runs for ye Wicket that is put down is Out. If they are not cross'd he that returns is Out.

Batt Foot or Hand over ye Crease

If in running a notch ye Wicket is struck down by a throw, before his foot hand or Batt is over ye popping Crease, or a stump hit by ye Ball though ye Bail was down, its Out. But if ye Bail is down before, he that catches ye Ball must strike a Stump out of ye Ground, Ball in hand, then its Out.

If ye Striker touches or takes up ye Ball before she is lain quite still unless asked by ye Bowler or Wicket-keeper, its Out.

When ye Ball has been in hand by one of ye Keepers or Stopers, and ye Player has been at home, He may go where he pleases till ye next ball is bowled.

If either of ye Strikers is cross'd in his running ground designedly, which design must be determined by the Umpires, N.B. The Umpire(s) may order that Notch to be scored.

When ye Ball is hit up, either of ye Strikers may hinder ye catch in his running ground, or if she's hit directly across ye wickets, ye other Player may place his body anywhere within ye swing of his Batt, so as to hinder ye Bowler from catching her, but he must neither strike at her nor touch her with his hands.

If a Striker nips a ball up just before him, he may fall before his Wicket, or pop down his Batt before she comes to it, to save it.

Ye Bail hanging on one Stump, though ye Ball hit ye Wicket, its Not Out.

Laws for Wicket Keepers

Ye Wicket Keepers shall stand at a reasonable distance behind ye Wicket, and shall not move till ye Ball is out of ye Bowlers hand, and shall not by any noise incommode ye Striker, and if his hands knees foot or head be over before ye Wicket, though ye Ball hit it, it shall not be Out.

Laws for ye Umpires

To allow 2 Minutes for each Man to come in when one is out, and 10 Minutes between each Hand.

To Mark ye Ball that it may not be changed.

They are sole judges of all Outs and Ins, of all fair and unfair play, of frivolous delays, of all hurts, whether real or pretended, and are discretionally to allow what time they think proper before ye Game goes on again.

In case of a real hurt to a Striker, they are to allow another to come in and ye Person hurt to come in again, but are not to allow a fresh Man to play, on either Side, on any Account.

BAT AND BALL

They are sole judges of all hindrances, crossing ye Players in running, and standing unfair to strike, and in case of hindrance may order a Notch to be scored.

They are not to order any Man out unless appealed to by one of ye Players.

(These Laws are to ye Umpires jointly.)

Each Umpire is sole judge of all Nips and Catches, Ins and Outs, good or bad Runs, at his own Wicket, and his determination shall be absolute, and he shall not be changed for another Umpire without ye consent of both Sides.

When 4 Balls are bowled, he is to call Over.

(These Laws are Separately.)

When both Umpires shall call Play, 3 times, 'tis at ye peril of giving ye Game from them that refuse to Play.

II

MODERN—1884 AND ONWARDS

1. A match is played between two sides of eleven players each, unless otherwise agreed to; each side has two innings, taken alternately except in the case provided for in Law 53. The choice of innings shall be decided by tossing.

2. The score shall be reckoned by runs. A run is scored:

    1st. So often as the batsmen after a hit, or at any time while the ball is in play, shall have crossed, and made good their ground, from end to end.

    2nd. For penalties under Laws 16, 34, 41, and allowances under 44.

Any run or runs so scored shall be duly recorded by scorers appointed for the purpose. The side which scores the greatest number of runs wins the match. No match is won unless played out or given up, except in the case provided in Law 45.

"ANCIENT AND MODERN"

3. Before the commencement of the match two **Umpires** shall be appointed; one for each end.

4. The Ball shall weigh not less than five ounces and a half, nor more than five ounces and three-quarters. It shall measure not less than eight and thirteen-sixteenth inches nor more than nine inches in circumference. At the beginning of each innings either side may demand a new ball.

(Note: In Instructions to Umpires it is laid down that after 200 runs have been made with a ball in the County Competition only, the fielding side can demand a new one.)

5. The Bat shall not exceed four inches and one-quarter in the widest part; it shall not be more than thirty-eight inches in length.

6. The Wickets shall be pitched opposite and parallel to each other at a distance of twenty-two yards. Each wicket shall be eight inches in width, and consist of three stumps with two bails upon the top. The stumps shall be of equal and sufficient size to prevent the ball passing through, twenty-seven inches out of the ground. The bails shall be each four inches in length, and when in position, on the top of the stumps, shall not project more than half an inch above them. The wickets shall not be changed during a match, unless the ground between them become unfit for play, and then only by consent of both sides.

7. The Bowling Crease shall be in a line with the stumps; eight feet eight inches in length; the stumps in the centre; with a return crease at each end, at right angles behind the wicket.

8. The Popping Crease shall be marked four feet from the wicket, parallel to it, and be deemed unlimited in length.

9. The Ground shall not be rolled, watered, mown, or

BAT AND BALL

beaten during a match, except before the commencement of each innings and of each day's play, when, unless the in-side object, the ground shall be swept and rolled for not more than ten minutes. This shall not prevent the batsman from beating the ground with his bat, nor the batsman nor bowler from using sawdust in order to obtain a proper foothold.

M.C.C.'s Note on Law 9.—The batting side has a right to have the ground swept and rolled " for not more than 10 minutes " before the commencement of each innings and of each day's play. It is the duty of the captain to see that his side obtain this advantage. The ground in this law means " the pitch."

The responsibility of supervising the rolling of the pitch before the play will, in the first place, rest with the umpires.

During the winter of 1924, the Committee of the M.C.C. approved the following recommendation of the Advisory Committee :

"*Any covering may be adopted to protect the whole of the pitch at any time after but not before 11 a.m. on the day immediately preceding until the time fixed for the match or until it begins, but in all cases where the whole of the wicket is so protected in a Saturday-start match, with the consent of the two captains, the same covering may be used throughout the succeeding Sunday. After the actual commencement of play the ground may again be protected when necessary and shall be protected every night during the continuation of a match, but the covering shall be removed each morning if fine, at 7 o'clock. The covering after the commencement of the match must not protect a larger area than 18 ft. by 12 ft. at each end and must not protect more than 3 ft. 6 in. in front of the popping crease, except on Sundays as previously provided for.*"

In the April of 1929 it was recommended as an experiment for all inter-county matches that a maximum of seven minutes actual rolling be made the rule instead of ten minutes. This

"ANCIENT AND MODERN"

was adopted and put into force as an experiment in the season of 1929 *and continued since.*

10. The ball must be bowled; if thrown or jerked either umpire shall call " No ball."

11. The bowler shall deliver with one foot on the ground behind the bowling crease, and within the return crease, otherwise the umpire shall call " No ball."

12. If the bowler shall bowl the ball so high over or so wide of the wicket that, in the opinion of the umpire, it is not within reach of the striker, the umpire shall call " Wide ball."

13. The ball shall be bowled in overs of six balls from each wicket alternately. When six balls have been bowled, and the ball is finally settled in the bowler's or wicket-keeper's hands, the umpire shall call " Over." Neither a " no ball " nor " wide ball " shall be reckoned as one of the " over."

14. The bowler shall be allowed to change ends as often as he pleases, provided only that he does not bowl two overs consecutively in one innings.

15. The bowler may require the batsman at the wicket from which he is bowling to stand on that side of it which he may direct.

16. The striker may hit a " no ball," and whatever runs result shall be added to his score; but he shall not be out from a " no ball " unless he be run out or break Laws 26, 27, 29, 30. All runs made from a " no ball " otherwise than from the bat shall be scored " no balls," and if no run be made one run shall be added to that score. From a " wide ball " as many runs as are run shall be added to the score, as " wide balls," and if no run be otherwise obtained one run shall be so added.

17. If the ball, not having been called " wide " or " no ball," pass the striker without touching his bat or person, and any runs be obtained, the umpire shall call " Bye ";

BAT AND BALL

but if the ball touch any part of the striker's person (hand excepted) and any run be obtained the umpire shall call "Leg bye," such runs to be scored "byes" and "leg byes" respectively.

18. At the beginning of the match, and of each innings, the umpire at the bowler's wicket shall call "Play," and from that time no trial ball shall be allowed to any bowler on the ground between the wickets, and when one of the batsmen is out, the use of the bat shall not be allowed to any person until the next batsman shall come in.

Note on Law 18.—In 1911 an agreement was arrived at between the Counties that "Trial balls, if both batsmen are at the wickets, be not allowed in first-class matches." This arrangement was approved and adopted by the M.C.C.

19. A batsmen shall be held to be "out of his ground," unless his bat in hand or some part of his person be grounded within the line of the popping crease.

20. The wicket shall be held to be "down" when either of the bails is struck off, or, if both bails be off, when a stump is struck out of the ground.

Umpires are now instructed to give a batsman out if the bail be out of the groove, always providing they are convinced that the ball had actually struck the stumps.

The STRIKER is out—

21. If the wicket be bowled down, even if the ball first touch the striker's bat or person :—"Bowled."

22. Or, if the ball, from a stroke of the bat or hand, but not the wrist, be held before it touch the ground, although it be hugged to the body of the catcher :—"Caught."

23. Or, if in playing at the ball, provided it be not touched by the bat or hand, the striker be out of his ground, and the wicket be put down by the wicket-keeper with the ball or with hand or arm, with ball in hand :—"Stumped."

"ANCIENT AND MODERN"

24. Or, if with any part of his person he stops the ball, which, in the opinion of the umpire at the bowler's wicket, shall have been pitched in a straight line from it to the striker's wicket and would have hit it :—" Leg before wicket."

It was decided in November 1934 that throughout 1935 a trial be given to an amended l.b.w. law, which reads : " The striker is out l.b.w. if with any part of his person (except his hand) which is between wicket and wicket he intercept a ball which, in the opinion of the umpire at the bowler's wicket, shall have been pitched in a straight line from the bowler's wicket to the striker's wicket or shall have been pitched on the offside of the striker's wicket and would have hit it.

25. Or, if in playing at the ball he hit down his wicket with his bat or any part of his person or dress :—" Hit wicket."

26. Or, if under pretence of running, or otherwise, either of the batsmen wilfully prevent a ball from being caught :— " Obstructing the field."

27. Or, if the ball be struck, or be stopped by any part of his person and he wilfully strikes it again, except it be done for the purpose of guarding his wicket, which he may do with his bat, or any part of his person except his hands : —" Hit the ball twice."

Either BATSMAN is out—

28. If in running, or at any other time, when the ball is in play, he be out of his ground, and his wicket be struck down by the ball after touching any fieldsman, or by the hand or arm, with ball in hand, of any fieldsman ; but the Striker may not be given out thus, unless the ball has touched the bat or hand, when in playing at a " no ball," he is out of his ground and the wicket be put down by the wicket-keeper with the ball, or with hand or arm with ball in hand :—" Run out."

29. Or, if he touch with his hands or take up the ball

BAT AND BALL

while in play, unless at the request of the opposite side :—
" Handled the ball."

30. Or, if he wilfully obstruct any fieldsman :—" Obstructing the field."

31. If the batsmen have crossed each other, he that runs for the wicket which is put down is out ; if they have not crossed, he that has left the wicket which is put down is out.

32. The striker being caught, no run shall be scored. A batsman being run out, that run which was being attempted shall not be scored.

33A. A batsman being out from any cause, the ball shall be " Dead."

33B. If the ball, whether struck with the bat or not, lodges in a batsman's clothing, the ball shall become " Dead."

34. If a ball in play cannot be found or recovered, any fieldsman may call " Lost ball," when the ball shall be " Dead " ; six runs shall be added to the score ; but if more than six runs have been run before " Lost ball " has been called, as many runs as have been run shall be scored.

35. After the ball shall have been finally settled in the wicket-keeper's or bowler's hand, it shall be " Dead " ; but when the bowler is about to deliver the ball, if the batsman at his wicket be out of his ground before actual delivery, the said bowler may run him out ; but if the bowler throw at that wicket and any run result, it shall be scored " No ball."

36. A batsman shall not retire from his wicket and return to it to complete his innings after another has been in, without the consent of the opposite side.

37. A substitute shall be allowed to field or run between wickets for any player who may, during the match, be incapacitated from illness or injury, but for no other reason, except with the consent of the opposite side.

"ANCIENT AND MODERN"

38. In all cases where a substitute shall be allowed, the consent of the opposite side shall be obtained as to the person to act as substitute and the place in the field which he shall take.

39. In case any substitute shall be allowed to run between wickets, the striker may be run out if either he or his substitute be out of ground. If the striker be out of his ground while the ball is in play, that wicket which he has left may be put down and the striker given out, although the other batsman may have made good the ground at that end, and the striker and his substitute at the other end.

40. A batsman is liable to be out for any infringement of the Laws by his substitute.

41. The fieldsman may stop the ball with any part of his person, but if he wilfully stop it otherwise, the ball shall be "Dead," and five runs added to the score; whatever runs may have been made, five only shall be added.

42. The wicket-keeper shall stand behind the wicket. If he shall take the ball for the purpose of stumping before it has passed the wicket, or if he shall incommode the striker by any noise, or motion, or if any part of his person be over or before the wicket, the striker shall not be out, excepting under Laws 26, 27, 28, 29, and 30.

43. The Umpires are the sole judges of fair or unfair play, of the fitness of the ground, the weather, and the light for play; all disputes shall be determined by them, and if they disagree the actual state of things shall continue.

44. They shall pitch fair wickets, arrange boundaries where necessary and the allowances to be made for them, and change ends after each side has had one innings.

45. They shall allow two minutes for each striker to come in, and ten minutes between each innings. When they shall call "Play," the side refusing to play shall lose the match.

BAT AND BALL

46. They shall not order a batsman out unless appealed to by the other side.

N.B.—An appeal, " How's that ? " covers all ways of being out (within the jurisdiction of the umpire appealed to), unless a specific way of getting out is stated by the person asking.

47. The umpire at the bowler's wicket shall be appealed to before the other umpire in all cases, except in those of stumping, hit wicket, run out at the striker's wicket, or arising out of Law 42, but in any case in which an umpire is unable to give a decision he shall appeal to the other umpire, whose decision shall be final.

48. If either umpire be not satisfied of the absolute fairness of the delivery of any ball, he shall call " No ball."

48A. The umpire shall take especial care to call " No ball " instantly upon delivery. " Wide ball " as soon as it shall have passed the striker.

49. If either batsman run a short run, the umpire shall call " One short," and the run shall not be scored.

50. After the umpire has called " Over " the ball is " Dead," but an appeal may be made as to whether either batsman is out ; such appeal, however, shall not be made after the delivery of the next ball nor after any cessation of play.

51. No umpire shall be allowed to bet.

52. No umpire shall be changed during a match, unless with the consent of both sides, except in case of violation of Law 51 ; then either side may dismiss him.

53. The side which bats first and leads by 150 runs in a three-day match, or by 100 runs in a two-day match, shall have the option of requiring the other side to follow their innings.

54. The in-side may declare their innings at an end in a three-day match at any time on the second day ; in a two-day match the captain of the batting side has

"ANCIENT AND MODERN"

power to declare his innings at a close at any time, but such declaration may not be made on the first day later than one hour and forty minutes before the time agreed upon for drawing stumps; in a one-day match at any time.

55. (Passed in 1914.) When there is no play on the first day of a three-day match, Laws 53 and 54 shall apply as if the match were a two-day match, and if in a three-day match there is no play on the first two days, Laws 53, 54, and Law 1, " one-day matches," shall apply as if the match were a one-day match.

(Addition passed in 1919.) When there is no play on the first day of a two-day match Law 1 " one-day matches" shall apply as if the match were a one-day match.

ONE-DAY MATCHES

1. The side which bats first and leads by 75 runs shall have the option of requiring the other side to follow their innings.

2. The match, unless played out, shall be decided by the first innings. Prior to the commencement of a match it may be agreed :—that the over consist of five or six balls.

N.B.—A Tie is included in the words " Played out."

THE NAMES

There's music in the names I used to know,
And magic when I heard them, long ago.
" Is Tyldesley batting ? "   Ah, the wonder still !
. . . The school-clock crawled, but cricket thoughts would
    fill
The last slow lesson-hour deliciously.
(Drone on, O teacher : you can't trouble me.)
" Kent will be out by now. . . ."   (Well, if you choose
To keep us here while cricket's in the air,
You must expect our minds to wander loose
Along the roads to Leicester, Lord's, and Leeds,
Old Trafford and The Oval, and the Taunton meads. . . .)

And then, at last, we'd raid the laneway where
A man might pass, perchance, with latest news.
Grey-grown and grave, yet he would smile to hear
Our thirsty questions as we crowded near.
Greedily from the quenching page we'd drink—
How its white sun-glare made our young eyes wink !
" Yes, Tyldesley's batting still.   He's ninety-four.
Marlow and Mold play well.   Notts win once more.
Gloster (with Grace) have lost to Somerset—
Easy : ten wickets : Woods and Palairet. . . ."

So worked the magic in that summer lane.
The stranger beamed.   Maybe he felt again
As I feel now, to tell the linkèd names
Jewelling the loveliest of our English games.

THE NAMES

Abel, and Albert Trott, Lilley, Lilywhite,
Hirst, Hearne, and Tunnicliffe—they catch the light—
Lord Hawke and Hornby, Jessop, A. O. Jones—
Surely the glow they held was the high sun's!

Or did a young boy's worship think it so,
And is it but his heart that's aching now?

THOMAS MOULT.